D0389862

Taking Theology
to Youth Ministry

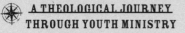

A THEOLOGICAL JOURNEY
THROUGH YOUTH MINISTRY

Taking Theology
to Youth Ministry

ANDREW ROOT

ZONDERVAN®
.com

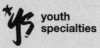

youth
specialties

ZONDERVAN.com/
AUTHORTRACKER
follow your favorite authors

ZONDERVAN

Taking Theology to Youth Ministry
Copyright © 2012 by Andrew Root

YS Youth Specialties is a trademark of YOUTHWORKS!, INCORPORATED and is
registered with the United States Patent and Trademark Office.

This title is also available as a Zondervan ebook.

Requests for information should be addressed to:

Zondervan, *Grand Rapids, Michigan 49530*

Library of Congress Cataloging-in-Publication Data

Root, Andrew, 1974-
    Taking theology to youth ministry / Andrew Root.
      p. cm.
    ISBN 978-0-310-67076-6 (hardcover)
    1. Church work with youth. 2. Church work. 3. Theology. I. Title.
BV4447.R657 2012
259'.23—dc23   2012008105

Cover design and cover art: SharpSeven Design
Interior design: Matthew Van Zomeren

Printed in the United States of America

12 13 14 15 16 17 18 /DCI/ 20 19 18 17 16 15 14 13 12 11 10 9 8 7 6 5 4 3 2 1

To Maisy
whose tenderness and humor melt me

Contents

Preface to a Peculiar Project

You're holding in your hand an experiment—a kind of dogmatic theology written through, and for, youth ministry. And by "dogmatic" I don't mean rigid, authoritarian, or inflexible, as the term is often used in popular language. Rather, I mean the heart—the essentials—of the church's teaching on God and God's work. When theologians throughout church history have set about to articulate the central theological ideas of our faith, they have often called it "dogmatics."

So what you hold is a dogmatic theology written through youth ministry. But this is an experiment because it is dogmatics written through youth ministry as a *narrative*, a fictional story of a youth worker named Nadia. Adding to the peculiarity of this theological project is the fact that it's *short*—each of the four books is just over 100 pages, meaning you should be able to read each in a sitting or two or three. (Which volume of Barth's *Church Dogmatics* allows for that?)

In many ways the best analogy for this series of books is

the energy bar. An energy bar is a small item, no bigger than a candy bar, but it serves as a meal. I hope these small books can satisfy your theological appetite; I hope that like an energy bar they will give you a protein-filled theological power-up to your concept and practice of youth ministry. But also like an energy bar (at least a quality one), I hope it tastes good—I hope the narrative shape is like a chocolate covering making the protein burst enjoyable.

These books continue a conversation—well, maybe even a kind of *movement*. I believe a small but growing (in numbers and depth) group of youth workers are ready, even yearning, to think theologically about youth ministry. Kenda Creasy Dean and I have called this development "the theological turn" in our book *The Theological Turn in Youth Ministry*. These books continue fleshing out this turn, hoping to give more depth and direction as we make this shift.

There are many to thank for this odd experiment you hold in your hand; acknowledging them all would make for too long a preface for such short books. But I'm compelled to thank a handful of people who directly impacted this work. First, thanks to Jay Howver, who heard about this project as just a wild idea over steak (a Zonder-steak, as I mockingly called those dinners). I thought I was only making conversation, but Jay called me the next week wanting to do the project. Jay's vision helped bring this weird idea to life.

I had a great editor in Doug Davidson. He worked tirelessly on this project, making it sing. I'm thankful for the support and skill he added to these books. I'd also like to thank Jess Daum for writing the wonderful discussion questions for each book. Jess has been one of my brightest students, and "Miss Jess" is also an enormous blessing to my whole family.

Jen Howver, too, deserves great thanks. I was overwhelmed with gratitude when she was assigned to title and set the marketing pack for these books. Jen is a dear friend, and it was a blessing to have these books in her talented hands. Plus, she's hated everything I've written before this—she thinks my writing is too academic. This gave me another shot to win her over! I think I did!

A number of people were kind enough to read versions of these books, providing major help and insight. My dear friend Blair Bertrand and the sharp-minded Erik Leafblad read book 1 (theology). One of my best former students, Tom Welch, and my colleague and friend Amy Marga (who saved me from grave error) read book 2 (the cross). One of my favorite youth workers and friends, Jon Wasson, and my dear colleague and running partner David Lose read book 3 (Scripture). And book 4 (mission and eschatology) was read by the deep-hearted and hilarious Spencer Edwards and the brilliant Christy Lang. Christy pushed me hard to rethink a number of perspectives and exegetical assertions; dealing with her feedback was exhausting and so helpful.

Finally, as always, I must thank Kara, my best friend and partner in all things. We started our friendship and love in our seminary days over summer Greek and Ray Anderson's lectures. I still vividly remember stopping into the Fuller library, reading sections of Barth's *Dogmatics,* and talking theology as we walked the streets of Pasadena. Our first intimate conversations were about theology. With her as my dialogue partner, I first learned to think theologically, parsing our way through "Ray" (as we called it) and discovering ourselves, each other, and God as we contemplated theology and Anderson's lectures. So it is to her that this project is offered in gratitude.

chapter one

The Chronicles of Nadia

The sweat fell from her forehead as Nadia heaved the last box from the cart into her new office. Sitting down to catch her breath, she wiped her brow and sighed deeply. This was it: Nadia's first full-time youth ministry job, a position that came not only with a livable salary and benefits but also with her own office. As she looked up at the empty walls, she felt both anticipation and fear. "Can I really do this?" she audibly asked herself.

Even though this was her first full-time position, Nadia was no newcomer to youth ministry. She'd grown up in a vibrant youth program in a large church, volunteered with middle-schoolers for three years during college, served as lead counselor at a camp for two summers, and worked part time for a para-church ministry while taking seminary classes immediately after finishing college. But this was her first full-time position. *I can't believe I'm actually starting a career*, she thought to herself as she rose from the box to start the tedious job of unpacking.

Nadia never thought she'd be a youth pastor. As a biology major, she'd always imagined she would either go to med school (although she began doubting this after the first semester of her sophomore year) or become a biology teacher. But here she was. She had no regrets. Youth ministry had somehow grabbed hold of her; she loved being with young people and felt alive when she entered into spiritual conversations with them. She loved the energy and excitement of the many youth ministry training events she'd gone to. Although she felt a little shocked that this was where her life had led, she knew, as she put each item away, that she was where she was supposed to be.

Nadia had heard about this job from a family friend who was serving on the search committee and suggested she apply. The church had about 500 members, and its youth ministry included 30 high school students and 50 sixth, seventh, and eighth graders. The church was part of a large mainline denomination, yet its members rarely used that tradition as any kind of identity marker. The congregation was a bit more conservative than others in the denomination, yet it felt little animosity toward the larger body. Even the limited denominational affiliation of this congregation was new for Nadia, since she'd grown up in a very large nondenominational church and had spent the last few years in the parachurch world. She told the search committee she knew very little about the polity and theological commitments of the denomination, but that seemed to be of little concern. "Just love our kids and God— that's all that matters to us," they told her.

As Nadia got to know the church better, she found it to be a relatively functional place. Sure, it had a few idiosyncrasies, but nothing too crazy. She was joining a staff that included a senior pastor, an associate pastor, a half-time children's minister, and a three-quarter-time music director. Nadia found Jerry, the senior pastor, to be incredibly welcoming—a real "people person" who became most alive in conversation with others. But at his core Jerry was a pragmatist with little concern with big theological or philosophical ideas. He wasn't immune to them, just too busy to concern himself with them. He always wanted to know what was next, what was happening, what new strategies would be used to reach the church's goals.

During Nadia's first week, Jerry burst into her office, welcomed her heartily, and then said, "So, are you coming up with any new models of youth ministry? What's new?" A few months later, after attending a pastor's retreat, Jerry rushed into Nadia's office (interrupting her on the phone), threw a flyer on her desk, and said in a loud stage whisper, "You've got to go to this conference, they're on to something, their ministry is exploding!"—and then disappeared just as quickly. Nadia really liked (and even trusted) Jerry, but she often found herself wide-eyed and out of breath after conversations with him.

The real thinker on the staff was Erica, the associate pastor. Jerry was a dynamic preacher, but many in the congregation found Erica's sermons much more thought-provoking. Erica and Jerry worked well together, but they were opposites. Erica always spoke in a measured way while Jerry stirred the church with his frantic energy; it seemed obvious to Nadia that if not for Erica, Jerry would risk propelling the ministry too close to the sun. Erica grounded things in her sensitivity, wisdom, and intellect.

If Jerry wanted the church's youth ministry to be part

of *the next big thing*, Erica gave the youth ministry little thought. It wasn't that she didn't see it as important; she simply wanted nothing to do with it. She and the previous youth pastor, Chad, had both started at the church seven years earlier. Erica and Chad had been seminary classmates, and Jerry convinced the church to hire both of them—one as an associate pastor and the other as youth pastor. Jerry knew Erica would fortify the ministry immensely, providing strength in areas where he was weakest. But previous associates had been involved with the youth ministry, and Erica wanted none of it. Both to secure Erica and to infuse the youth ministry with professional expertise, Jerry pushed for the hiring of Chad as well.

Erica and Chad had worked closely together—even though Chad lived for youth ministry, and Erica couldn't stand it. But Erica could see that Chad was being eaten alive by youth ministry. Not only did Chad feel pressure from Jerry that Erica never experienced, but he also put huge pressure on himself. Chad saw it as his calling to invest in each kid's life, getting every student to understand the love of God and participate deeply in the ministry. He was always rushing from one activity to another. Chad stuck it out for seven years, but when he finally quit, he left ministry altogether to take a job as a manager of his father-in-law's carpet business. So while Jerry presented Nadia with flyers promoting the next big thing, Erica spoke often of her concern that youth ministry, like a caged beast, eats anyone ignorant enough to wrestle with it. Nadia found herself wedged between ambitious Jerry, who hoped the youth ministry would glitter, and skeptical Erica, who was convinced that a lot of the glitter was anything but gold.

In the first few months of her new job, Nadia wasn't concerned about Jerry and Erica's differing perspectives. She had no time to seek the next big thing; she needed to attend to immediate concerns that demanded her attention. As for skepticism, there was no time for that, either. It was time to get going; the church expected her to resurrect the youth ministry from Chad's burnout and move it somewhere different, somewhere beyond where it was now. For some church members, this meant exponential growth in the number of church kids attending ministry events; for others, it meant reaching into the surrounding community to open the youth ministry beyond kids whose parents went to the church. Nadia figured her experience with the parachurch had assured them she knew something about this.

Nadia began to realize that while both groups agreed the youth ministry needed to grow, their ideas of growth set them into two distinct camps. One camp was parents, elders, and congregation members who often said things like, "We want a youth ministry like we had here a few decades ago, when kids loved coming." Soon after Nadia took the job, a couple of parents cornered her and explained how excited they were that she'd joined the staff, adding that they hoped she would make the youth ministry more appealing to their children. "I just loved youth group when I was a kid," said one parent, "but my kids hate it. They say it's boring. The church across town has loads of kids, and they do so many fun things! Are you going to do stuff like that?"

Nadia nodded in response, because she *did* want to do fun things, and she wanted the youth to enjoy being part of the group. But she could feel hesitation creeping up her spine, because she knew that creating a meaningful youth program was much more complicated than providing lots of fun stuff to do. After all, Chad's ministry corpse was buried under a million fun activities.

The other camp seemed just as passionate, speaking of the need for evangelism and outreach. They weren't as concerned with fun as with significance. They pictured a youth group where kids were growing as disciples both in knowledge and action: "We want kids within the community to come to know Jesus and for those kids as well as the kids in our church to live out their faith in service." Nadia wanted this, too—she'd given the last few years to such activity in the parachurch world. But she knew this was no easy task. As she listened to their concerns, she could feel her own apprehensiveness; in the heat of their zeal, her own questions rose so quickly that Nadia bit the tip of her tongue to keep them from spilling out. She imagined that Chad had drowned trying to navigate these currents, just swimming harder instead of facing the force of these questions.

It soon became clear to Nadia that she'd have to be able to explain the reasons for whatever she was doing. Both camps would want justification for the actions she took. The difficulty was that the justification for the shape of the ministry would have to be anchored to something—something other than "success," because these camps defined *success* differently.

Nadia knew Chad had joined the church staff right out of seminary. Even though she had not completed seminary, it was clear from her very first job interview that some members of the church really valued her year and a half of seminary experience. Nadia found this both ironic and serendipitous, because she'd gone to seminary only because the parachurch ministry she'd been working with had offered to pay for half of it; she'd found little of it interesting and almost none of it helpful. She was relieved when the church agreed it would be better if she put seminary on hold as she started this new endeavor, although they wanted her to continue in a semester or two. Erica believed seminary was essential (Nadia figured this was because Erica didn't see youth ministry as a final ministerial destination), and Jerry thought seminary was a good idea—he'd read that longevity and depth as a youth minister were correlated with a seminary education. Nadia agreed that continuing seminary made sense, but deep down she hoped the others would forget. It wasn't that Nadia wasn't smart enough; she found seminary very do-able, it just seemed so disconnected from, and irrelevant to, her work with the youth. Even the elements she liked, she found hard to relate to her ministry. Plus, Chad had completed seminary—and now he was selling carpet.

After just eight months on the job, Nadia already felt a real connection to the young people in the ministry. She'd taken the kids on a mission trip, began a weekly Bible study, and gave a talk at each weekly youth group meeting. She'd been told her job was to build a youth ministry, but Nadia felt more moved by the young people themselves than by the task of constructing an infrastructure. When she thought of her ministry, it wasn't the calendar or mission statement that rushed to her mind, but the faces of kids like Jared, the slightly overweight seventh grader who sat quietly against the wall until he was approached. Nadia's heart almost broke in two when she asked Jared how he liked his new school, and he blinked back tears before saying with a choked-up voice, "I don't have many friends there." Nadia thought of Kelsey, the skinny-as-a-rail eighth grader who dressed in black and had issues with food and at home. And Nadia thought about

Kelsey's sister Kammie who seemed to be the perfect junior—pretty, outgoing, academically and athletically successful, a leader in every way. She thought of the studious Tim who missed all the group's activities in November to study for his SAT retake. She thought of so many more.

Nadia walked into the room for her first-year evaluation with both confidence and apprehension. Her apprehension revolved around having to face all the distinct people and diverse perspectives in one room. Not only would both Jerry and Erica be present but also representatives from each of the two camps of parents. Their first question caught her completely off guard. It really shouldn't have; anyone could have seen it coming, and she'd even considered it herself. But its verbalization sent her into deep thought, mostly circling around how she could even begin to articulate her answer. She found herself saying something, though it was as if she were standing outside herself listening, even as her mind continued to grasp for what she really meant to say. But she just kept talking.

Apparently, her answer was acceptable. They moved on to another question, but she never did. Her being had grasped on to that very first question and would not let it go. She continued in the conversation, even as the first question continued ringing like a siren in the background of her thoughts.

It was a basic question, a fundamental question, but everything hinged on it. They had asked, *"What's the purpose of this youth ministry?"* And Nadia knew what the review committee may not have known: She needed to have a clear answer to this question, or she'd be pushed by the winds of everyone else's expectations and desires—or, worse, she'd be eaten up by the same burnout beast that had devoured Chad.

chapter two

What's It All About?

Nadia's first-year evaluation went very well. She was affirmed and rewarded with a bigger continuing education budget and a 7 percent salary raise. But the committee's first question remained with her, it sat heavy in her lap. But it was not a burden; rather, it cajoled her to search for its answer, and she believed that finding that answer might radically change her ministry, if not her very self. After the meeting she sat in her office staring at the youth ministry calendar on the wall contemplating the question, "What's the purpose of youth ministry?"

In the last four decades youth ministry has become *something*. It has become a common operation of many congregations (most local churches have or wish to have youth ministries), it has become a profession (with degrees, certificates, and manuals), it has become a market (with events, products, and outings), and it has become a field of academic study (with journals, professors, and departments). Youth ministry has sent colorful flares into the sky of the church world to announce that it has arrived and can't be ignored. But like a fireworks show in mid-April, all the color and noise leaves many of us wondering about its purpose.

It's not that youth ministry has never been concerned about purpose. Like all maturing movements, youth ministry has gradually given more and more attention to efficiency and productivity. It has made strong assertions about the need to be purpose-driven, to operate from a purpose. Many have talked about how important it is for youth ministry to be *intentional.* Whatever our ministry philosophy is—whether we seek to be leader-based, program-based, family-based, relationship-based, peer-based, or whatever—it's important that we be intentional. And I agree; it is important to be clear about our intentions, and to do ministry from them.

MORE THAN INTENTIONS

But too often we've assumed that intentions and purpose are one and the same. We think that if we're clear about our intentions—if we know what it is we want to accomplish—then we've also fully defined our purpose. And we believe that as long as our intentions are clear and focused, our purpose will be direct (and even pure). So if we are asked, "What is your intention for this youth ministry?" we might answer, "My intention is that every kid comes to know Jesus, follow Jesus, and serve Jesus." We say that's our intention, and then we do whatever it is we do in hopes of making that happen. Or, as one youth pastor once told me, "I'm in the disciple-making business—and I use youth ministry to do that." His intention, the goal he is seeking to accomplish, is clear—he wants to make disciples. In Nadia's initial interview for the job, this is how she heard the question, "What do you think the purpose of youth ministry is?" She heard it as, "What are your intentions for this group of young people?" She answered by telling what she planned to do with them—Bible studies, mission trips, service projects, etc.

But there's more to purpose than just intentions, what we hope to accomplish. Purpose is our intentions in connection (or disconnection) to our motives. While our intentions usually live more explicitly on the surface of our actions, our motives live more implicitly within us. I might talk a lot about my intentions, but my motive, that which I'm motivated by, will have huge impact on how I actually act.

A father might ask his daughter's boyfriend, "What are your intentions with my daughter?" In other words: What are you planning on doing with her? Marrying her? Using her? Living with her? What are your plans? The boyfriend responds that his intention is to marry her someday—at least that's what he tells himself, his girlfriend, and her father. His intentions might be noble, but his motivations—his true reason for acting— might feel much less so. Maybe he finds himself motivated more by the desire of having an intimate sexual relationship with her. His intention is to put a ring on her finger—at least that's what he tells himself—but his motives aren't in line with his intentions. And when he never gets around to popping the question, he can assert his innocence because he always "intended" to do so. But the reason he never accomplished this was because his true motives weren't in line with his intentions.

As a youth pastor, my intention is to love every kid for who he or she is. But at a deeper, perhaps even unconscious level, my motivation might be to see the kids I work with showing outward indications that their faith is growing, because that will prove that my ministry is a success. And in such a situation, there will be times where my intentions (to love every kid for who they are) get trampled by my motivation (to see signs of growth in kids, whether in their prayer life or acts of social justice). We often try to smother our motives, never honestly acknowledging or wrestling with them, perhaps hoping that if we can be clear in stating our intentions, then our motives don't really need to be dealt with.

But when the evaluation committee asked Nadia about the purpose of youth ministry, for the first time, she heard this question not as, "What is your intention?" but, "What is your motivation?" She knew what her intentions were with the ministry. She intended to respect the kids and help them grow in faith by participating in the activities and relationships the ministry provided. In fact, those intentions are what got her the job (and that's probably why her rambling answer seemed sufficient to the committee). But sitting in that hard chair at her first-year evaluation, she realized she had no idea what her motivation *really* was. What was at her core that compelled her into ministry? From the place of motivation, what was youth ministry for?

I think many of us share the same intentions in youth ministry. In one way or another, most of us intend to encourage young people to love and serve God, and we intend to love and support them. Even the most ideologically driven liberals and conservatives can find some commonality in these intentions. Their differences are often more a matter of their motivation. For example, it's not uncommon for youth groups from both liberal and conservative congregations to participate on the same mission trips in collaboration with a group like Youth-works! Both youth groups intend to spend a week of service, traveling across the Mexican border to help build and paint a house for a family there. But all week they're skeptical of each other. The liberals wonder if the conservatives are working on the house simply as a way of winning leverage to evangelize. And the conservatives imagine the liberals are motivated by an ideology of inclusive do-goodism that has no room for sin or Jesus. Even when they agree about *what* they are doing (intentions), each distrusts the other's *why* (motivation). And I contend that this is because intentions are the skin of purpose, but motivations are its heart.

When we keep the conversation about the purpose of youth ministry at the level of intentions, our motives too often remain hidden, and this keeps them from the light of theological reflection. We assume we're doing theology because we can use theological language to express our intentions, but this theological language is only a candy-coated shell that gives the impression that we've thought theologically about youth ministry. But real theology moves past the surface and calls us to wrestle with the heart of our motives, as Jacob wrestled the angel (Genesis 32). Theology is only theology when it becomes dangerous, when it threatens to leave us limping by exposing our motives to the action of God. Too much purpose-driven theological reflection in youth ministry has been more fodder for candy shops than dangerous wrestling, because it views theology as a bunch of biblical bullet points used to sweeten our intentions, rather than a call to examine our motives in light of God's judgment and grace.

It's only when our motives are dragged from their darkness, only when we wrestle with them until the break of dawn, that we are taking a deeply theological turn, that we are demanding a blessing, and that theology places us near the action of God, giving our motives a new name next to the promise of God. Or, to say it another way, it is only after we've reflected on our motives that we have allowed theology to bless our purpose.

I'm not suggesting that theology and Bible study haven't been part of our purpose driven-ness in youth ministry. But when purpose is viewed only as intentions and never goes to the level of motives, which has happened too often in youth ministry, then theological reflection is limited to flat, stale biblical assertions given to us in easily digestible sound bytes. When our purpose is no more than our intentions, then theology is only used to justify (proof text) our intentions. So we have to ask again, "What is youth ministry for?"—pushing the question beyond intention into conversations about motivation.

THE MOTIVATION FOR YOUTH MINISTRY

When we look at the purpose of youth ministry at the level of our motivations, we can see a number of hidden or implicit purposes that drive many youth programs. In many cases, these purposes have little to do with, or maybe even conflict with, our theological commitments.

Keeping Kids Good

Maybe the most driving motivation of many youth ministries has been to keep kids good. Of course, few youth workers would state that their core purpose, the reason their ministries exist, is to keep kids safe or moral. This sounds too much like baby-sitting or being the moral police. That's not the primary goal of most youth workers. In fact, most people would agree it's quite possible to keep kids "good" without ever acknowledging the presence of God in the world. Most would assert, from the location of their intentions, that they want kids to be good because such "goodness" grows out of following Jesus. But in the end, creating good kids is not what youth ministry is all about.

Although keeping kids good may not be our primary intention, too often it functions as a driving motivation. We make assessments about our ministry in light of this motive. And in doing so, we communicate that what ultimately matters is how good kids can be, that the purpose of Christianity is about being good—not lying, cheating, stealing, and having sex. The more "good kids" we have in our youth group, the more successful we think we are.

Eric is the youth pastor of a medium-sized church. When I asked him about his youth group, Eric said, "They're great kids. They really take their faith seriously. We have a handful of kids who refused to go to prom because of the drinking and explicit dancing. Our kids are just really serious about their faith." Lindsey has had the opposite experience with the youth at her church: "I don't know what we're doing wrong," she told me. "They just act one way at church and another at school." Eric feels things are going well because his motivation of keeping kids good is being met, while Lindsey feels like a failure.

While there are surely important ethical implications to our faith, ultimately, Christian discipleship is not about what we can make ourselves (or our kids) into, but about how God acts on our behalf. Even in a more Wesleyan tradition where holiness is central, the holiness we seek to embody is not something we obtain for ourselves, but a reality God calls us into, a response to God's action. Throughout the biblical narrative, God chooses to call those who seem to have a hard time being good—whether it's Jacob the con man (Genesis 25), Moses the murderer (Exodus 2), Ruth the liar (Ruth 3), David and Solomon the womanizers (2 Samuel 11), Mary the teenage mother (Matthew 1), or Paul the persecutor (Acts 8:1). The Bible is not an ethical textbook, but the story of God's actions among us—actions that reveal who God is and what God is up to in the world.

As she sat in her office pondering what youth ministry was for, Nadia realized she'd often been motivated by kids' behavior, thinking her ministry was successful because kids were behaving, because they were staying out of trouble. She never would have said her purpose was to keep kids good, but she began to realize this was a hidden motive that had shaped her ministry in substantial ways. She realized that keeping kids good was inadequate motivation for ministry. Not only did it too easily miss the difficulty of some young people's lives, but it also seemed to miss something about who God is.

Involving Kids in Service

A second driving motivation for many youth pastors is to involve kids in service. We want kids to own their faith, to participate in it. Often, this intention gets lived out in our attempts to have kids do things (build houses, write letters to Congress, serve lunch at a soup kitchen, etc). In a hyper-consumeristic context where kids are sold things at every turn, having them serve instead of being served is our goal.

Again, there is little doubt that faith in the God of Jesus Christ calls us to service, to actions of love for our neighbor. But too often we become so focused on this that we think the goal of youth ministry is to make kids into servants. A youth pastor once told me, "The purpose of our ministry is service. We've got kids out doing service projects every week. I can name dozens of kids that have been changed from consumers to servants, and now they are out working to make the world a better place because of our ministry."

But as Jesus said, no servant is greater than his master (John 15:20). And too often while our intention is to have kids serve so they might be near to God, our deeper motivation is to involve as many kids as possible in service work because it helps *us* feel like we're making a difference, like our ministry is important. Jesus himself was not motivated by service in general, but only by following his Father. ("The Son can do nothing by himself; he can do only what he sees his Father doing." John 5:19) Jesus passed on many service opportunities, and asserted that the ones he took were those his Father led him into. Jesus' motivation was not service in general, but rather to bend his life into the action of God, to participate in what God was doing, to be in relationship with his Father. He was a servant to his Father, not a servant to service.

Nadia did intend to get kids to reach out to others and serve the world. But slouching in her office chair, she recognized this couldn't be her motive—the real reason she did youth ministry. If calling kids to serve were her purpose, it would become a treadmill she could never get off of. "How much would be enough service?" she asked herself. "Enough that I feel like I'm doing a good job? Enough that I would feel like I'm making a difference in the world through these kids?" She could turn the youth group into a sweatshop that produced service as a pill for her own insecurity. Surely, that wasn't the goal.

Nadia remembered the story of the woman who'd anointed Jesus' feet with oil that was worth a full year's wages

(John 12:1–11). The disciples had criticized the woman, believing her act to be a wasteful use of resources that could have been used to meet other needs. But Jesus had called the woman's act a blessing, because she was participating in God's work. She was preparing Jesus' body for death. What mattered wasn't service itself, but participating in God's activity in the world (which, in the end, as we'll see in book four, is the real meaning of *service*).

Passing on the Tradition

A third motivation driving many youth ministries is passing on the elements of our faith tradition to kids. Depending on the particular church, this may be fleshed out in efforts to make young people more biblically centered or more rooted in a particular denomination or congregation. In my part of the country it's not uncommon to hear youth workers talk about the importance of making sure kids continue coming to church after they've been confirmed. So, if they have the budget, they use extravagant youth rooms and tons of events to convince youth that it is worth their time to stay committed to church.

Often, this persuasion is rooted in a desire to give kids a religious tradition to stand on in a secular world. Some youth programs are motivated by the idea of young people knowing the Bible and being able to quote it. "We're all about biblical knowledge," said one youth pastor. "Some ministries are about flash and entertainment, but our purpose is to see kids know the Bible and live like the Bible says."

Nadia had felt pressure from people in her church who had similar feelings. They kept telling her it was most important that kids know the Bible and become committed to the congregation and its denomination. But this never convinced

Nadia. Her experience with the parachurch made her hesitant to make commitment to any particular tradition a primary goal. As she shifted in her chair, still staring at the youth ministry calendar, she began to wonder if maybe these parents were right. Maybe passing on the tradition and its rich heritage should be the motive. She understood that tradition was powerful, and that Christian faith has a history that is important. The Bible is, of course, central to it. But she knew that there was a downside to such a focus. She knew that it's possible to make adherence to a particular tradition so central, so motivating, that there would be little reason for God at all. As long as kids had the tradition, and even the Bible, they wouldn't ever need to encounter the living God who is larger than any tradition. Nadia thought to herself: "Am I really supposed to make my youth group into a Pharisee factory, building smart, committed kids who will see it as their job to protect a tradition? That can't be what it's all about!"

THE PROBLEM OF PROFESSIONALIZATION

The professionalization of youth ministry has pushed us to be clear about purpose, to make our intentions known. There is much that's positive about this. But maybe a problem created by this professionalization is that it encourages us to ignore our motives, as opposed to actually doing ministry from the location of our motives, from the core of our own being. We get confused into thinking the heart of youth ministry is organized calendars and vision statements rather than having the courage to seek to become a part of God's action in the world, which always exposes our motives.

This realization is what hit Nadia with force during her first-year evaluation; she realized that her purpose (in the way she'd always understood it) had little to do with her heart and how she encountered God. She realized that she could be purpose-driven in youth ministry, getting all the marks of professional success, without ever exposing her motives to the judgment and grace of God. She found it ironic that the more she focused on being purpose-driven in youth ministry, the more God seemed frozen and unmoving. In the glow of professionalization, she was directed to focus on *her* intentions, making her hopes for the ministry direct and purposeful. She wasn't encouraged to see God as an actor until she moved the conversation into her motives, because her motives rested in a place very close to her own fear and insecurities—a place that needs confession, for-giveness, and the kind of transformation into a new way of being that only God can bring.

With her head in her hands, now leaning forward in her office chair, she realized for the first time that youth ministry wasn't a biblical concept or even a theological idea. Youth min-istry had only been a part of the church for the last hundred years or so, and had existed in its present form only for the last four or five decades. Youth ministry developed due to cultural reasons more than theological ones, because we have societal institutions like the high school that divide age cohorts into a group that then forms a distinct culture and a marketing niche. Youth ministry developed largely in response to these cultural realities more than any particular theological need.

But that doesn't mean there is nothing theological about youth ministry, only that it is all the more important that we expose not only our intentions but also our motives to the light of theological reflection. So with her head still in her hands she asked again: If youth ministry isn't for keeping kids good, for making them into servants, or for passing on a tradition, what is youth ministry for?

THE DRAMA

As that question bounced from one side of her brain to the other, there was a knock on the door. It was Mrs. Davis, the mother of Amanda, a high school junior who'd disappeared from the youth group over the last few months. "Am I interrupting anything?" Mrs. Davis asked in a bubble-gummy, upbeat voice, as she poked her head around the office door, a smile painted on her face.

Shaking the contemplative cobwebs from her mind, Nadia responded a little too energetically, "No! Not at all. Come in."

Mrs. Davis's polite disposition changed as she sat down. Before Nadia even had time to shift her full attention from the question she'd been considering, Mrs. Davis launched in with force. "I'm very upset with the youth group—very, very . . ." she trailed off, as her emotions started to wear on her face, revealing the creases in her cheeks that witnessed to her incessant smiling. Nadia's first thought was how weird it was to see Mrs. Davis without her trademark smile. Her drooping checks were as shocking as the words coming from her mouth.

"What's the problem?" Nadia asked, truly unaware of what the issue could be.

"It's Amanda. She hates coming to church," said Mrs. Davis. "And that just breaks my heart, because when I was her age I *loved* church, I loved youth group, I loved it all. But now she won't even go."

"Did she say why?" Nadia asked, both curious and also wanting to show compassion for this parent's pain.

"She says it's *boring!*" Mrs. Davis fired back, as if she were dropping a bomb in the middle of Nadia's office floor. As she said this, her head snapped back as if to protect herself from the coming explosion, having set off a charge of condemnation no youth worker could survive. Watching Mrs. Davis's reaction, Nadia remained silent at first, feeling little impact from the supposed bomb.

"I'm sorry to hear that," Nadia finally said, breaking the silence. "But I wonder if there is something more . . ." she continued.

But Mrs. Davis had no time for this change of conversational direction: "No," she interrupted, "I'm sure that's it, because she's started going to Ignite." Ignite was the name of the youth ministry at the large nondenominational congregation across town.

"Well, that's good—isn't it?" Nadia returned.

Mrs. Davis just shrugged. After a few seconds of silence, Mrs. Davis pressed her lips together and slowly nodded: "Well, I'm glad she's still involved in a church. But it still makes me upset, because I love this church. The whole reason we hired you was to form a group where the kids in this church would really feel like they belonged, a place they'd really want to come." Nadia knew Mrs. Davis was solidly in the camp of elders and parents who wanted her to make the youth group something fun that their kids would enjoy.

Nadia sat in silence for a few seconds, considering how to respond. When she finally spoke, her words were surprising, even to herself. "Well, that *is* an issue. We definitely want kids to feel like they can find a place here. *But* in the end, Mrs. Davis, I don't think youth ministry is for entertaining kids, or making them like church, or even for keeping them good or moral." As the words left her lips, Nadia breathed a quick shallow breath, because now she'd dropped her own bomb, almost without conscious intention. "Where did that come from?" she thought to herself.

Nadia could see the confusion in Mrs. Davis's face as the words hit her. She responded with narrowed eyes, leaning forward, "Then what is youth ministry for, Nadia?"

chapter three

Youth Ministry as Participation in God's Action

Nadia spent the next school year in deep personal reflection. She continued to consider the question, What is youth ministry for? She came to believe that it *couldn't* be for keeping kids good, making them exemplary servants, or passing on a tradition—and it surely wasn't all about keeping them entertained. Then what was it for? What was the core of what she was up to in ministry?

Nadia knew even back in her initial interview for the job that she would need to give some justification for what she'd be doing in ministry; even then, she could already feel competing pressures from multiple individuals and groups—Mrs. Davis, to name just one. To survive, she'd need to have some idea why she was doing what she was doing. Yet she'd been confident that once she began planning activities and working with kids, it would all become clear. She wasn't expecting to be knocked down by the depth of the purpose question; she wasn't prepared to wrestle with what she was doing in her ministry at the level of her very motivations. Thinking about ministry at this level meant her person was deeply involved in any answer she gave for the reason for youth ministry.[1] It seemed to widen her view of reality itself, moving her beyond what she wanted to accomplish and into the question of what she was called to do, beyond the reality of pizza and games and into a reality of mystery and transcendence—a reality where God moves.

And this, then, points to the real answer to the question Nadia was wrestling with. If youth ministry isn't about keeping kids good, making them into something, or passing something on, then what is it all about? I contend that at its core youth ministry is about participating in God's own action. The purpose of youth ministry is to invite both young and old to participate in God's action. Youth ministry, like all ministry, seeks in humility to be swept up into God's own action, and therefore to participate in God's activity in our world.

Youth ministry is no different from any other ministry in finding its very center in God's own act; where it is

---

1. When I refer to "person" throughout this series (i.e., to Nadia's person), I mean something different from "individual"—something more existential and relational. Thomas and Rosita Rourke state it well: "Ideologies left and right claim to be in favor of the 'individual,' and few have come to understand the fundamental difference between this 'individual' and the real human person. The concept of individual is distinctively modern and abstract. Although attempting to build on the moral capital accumulated by its predecessor, the person, it is different in kind. The person is concrete, historically and culturally situated, and a member of a specific community. The modern individual is detached from all of these connections." *A Theory of Personalism* (Lanham, MD: Lexington Books, 2005), p. x.

distinctive is only in its cultural location. *Youth ministry could be defined as the ministry of the church that seeks to participate in God's action with and for a culturally identified group called adolescents.* What this means in the end is that youth ministry is every bit as theological as every other form of ministry, because its core isn't games and skits but the action of God. What makes it distinct from other ministries is its particular focus on the actions of God *with and for young people.*

When we place the act of God as central, and participation in the action of God as the purpose for youth ministry, then every other motive for doing youth ministry must be put to death. I know this sounds dramatic, but stick with me. All other motives must be put to death, because there can be only one motive. (Kierkegaard would say, "The purity of the heart is to will only one thing"; Jesus would say, "Seek first [and finally] the kingdom of God," Matthew 6:33). The one motive for ministry is to participate in the act of God. Any other motive that does not have its origin in the act and being of God must be put to death. When God acts, all other motives must come under the judgment of God.

Consider the account in the book of Acts in which Philip meets Simon the Magician in Samaria (Acts 8:3-25). Simon is a powerful man who is magically able to do signs and wonders. But when Philip shows up, Simon's magic pales in comparison to the power of the resurrected Christ. Even magic must bend knee to the action of God. Infatuated by what he sees, Simon begins to follow Philip, believing Philip to be an even more powerful magician. But Simon is confused: Philip is no magician. Philip is a disciple, a follower and participant in the action of God. Philip possesses no magical power, just a heart that yearns to be part of God's actions. After baptizing some of the locals, Peter and John are called to lay hands on the people so that they might receive the Spirit. When Simon the magician sees this, he is both captivated and further confused. He wants the power to distribute the Spirit—wrongly believing this is what Peter and John are doing. Offering a significant amount of money to have these distribution rights, Simon is rebuked.

Simon the magician seeks to control God's activity, believing that with enough money he can make God's action into a commodity he can distribute or withhold. Simon believes God is inert and can be awakened by the right incantation—like a lawnmower that remains frozen until you pull the cord. Simon thinks his actions are what set God in motion. But the disciples know differently. This God of Jesus is a mover, a God who comes upon us without warning, behind closed doors with flames of fire. Simon wants to bring forth the Holy Spirit; but Philip, Peter, and John know that *no one* brings forth the Spirit—God comes when and where God comes. Simon is motivated by the idea of power and control, of what the ability to call forth God's Spirit might mean for his own actions. Ultimately, he is not interested in God's action as seen in the coming of the Spirit—for when God's action comes, it often reveals our own weakness (as we will see below), calling us into participation not through our strength but through our yearning and need.

Too often we youth workers function like Simon. We earnestly want the Spirit to come, but we spend all our time focusing on how we might distribute it to young people. We wonder what new magical model or program we might use to awaken God. We spend so much time focusing on our own purpose-driven ministry activities that we lose sight of our ultimate purpose—to participate in God's own action. And God's action comes most often by revealing our weakness, by moving in the places of our deepest yearning.

A youth worker once spoke with me about his feeling that youth ministry was an uphill battle, given the secular and consumerist tendencies of culture. But he felt like his efforts would all be worth it if just one kid got it, if just one kid received the Spirit and committed his or her life to God. The exhaustion in his face signaled that he had worked hard honing his technique so that *his actions* might distribute God to kids. But this tendency more closely resembles the thinking of Simon the magician than that of the disciples. Simon hopes that with the right technique and information he can learn to bring forth the Spirit, to assure that at least one person will "get it"—and he's willing to pay big money for this technique and information. But the disciples function in a different way. They seek to live into an altogether new reality, a reality where God moves. Peter and John are only called to Samaria because God is already moving. Their motive is singular; it is to participate in the act of God.

Abraham and Sarah had a motive, one they were confident came from God (Genesis 11–12). They sought to become a nation. But, of course, there was one problem. Sarah, the mother of this nation-to-be, was barren—and there could be no nation without children. So with the motivation of God's promise (to make Abraham into a nation), and the knowledge that Sarah was *way* past childbearing years, Abraham and Sarah acted, and did so in a way that was morally acceptable in their cultural context. Abraham slept with Hagar, the concubine, seeking to use her as the vessel to meet God's purpose. Hagar became the incantation that Abraham and Sarah hoped would awaken God.

Hagar gives birth to a son, Ishmael. But when Ishmael is thirteen years old, after thirteen years of being told he is God's promise, God acts—and God's actions put to death the motives and intentions of Abraham and Sarah. The judgment of God rings in their ears: Ishmael is not the promise, for Ishmael is the product of humans who sought to act in God's stead. God reminds this couple that there can only be one motive for ministry, and that motive is to participate in God's own action. In doing so, they become part of a reality where from death—the death of Sarah's barren womb—comes life.

It is not about what we do, but what God does among us. Too often, we get caught up in trying to eliminate our human weaknesses, seeking a fertile concubine to cover the disgrace of our barrenness. But the God of the covenant is a God who chooses our weakness as the location of God's action. God chooses the weakest people to be God's people. Barren wombs bring forth the promise, little shepherd boys become kings, and a cross of death brings eternal life.

To say that youth ministry's purpose is to participate in the act of God is no small statement. When God acts, God puts to death and brings to life—or, as Martin Luther often said, "God first kills before God makes alive." God moves at the deepest level of life and death; just as no one can see God's face and live (Exodus 33:20), no one can participate in the activity of God without being put to death. To say that participation in God's activity is the reason for youth ministry is to place youth ministry on dangerous ground (much more dangerous ground than having purpose-driven intentions). It is to place youth ministry on holy ground, it is to make youth ministry for participating in the God who encounters us in the empty space of our lives. It is to place the purpose of youth ministry within sight of the God whom no one can see and still live.

Too often youth ministry has been about accomplishing something—building a group, holding a conference, converting young people. But these are the actions of Simon and Hagar—attempts to call forth the Spirit and fulfill God's promises through our own efforts. We become fixated on what we are doing, thinking that if we can get our actions right, we will awaken God. This is why so much theological language surrounding youth ministry has focused on justifying our own activity, and so little has been about articulating how God acts, and who this God of action is. This misguided focus is the reason youth ministry has a poor theological reputation. But like all ministry, youth ministry is fundamentally a theological task, because it is about participating in God's action.

God is not concerned with fixing or getting past Sarah's barrenness, but acting from it, acting for new possibilities next to the impossibility she has carried as a heavy burden. To be swept up into God's action, to minister from the womb of Sarah rather than of Hagar, is to do ministry as weak and frail human beings, with the sole motivation of participating in God's act of love for young people.

Nadia felt convicted, as if God's judgment were contained in the question of what youth ministry is for. She saw that her efforts to encourage discipleship and service-learning were just the ministry of Hagar, youth ministry done from the place of her own power and control, a place that quickly divides motives and intentions.

ACTING FROM JUDGMENT AS GRACE

It's not just that the action of God tends to move from the location of our emptiness. In fact, God often uses our emptiness as the pathway into God's own action. In other words, it is our own emptiness that enables us to participate in God's action. This means that judgment (our emptiness) and grace (God's action) are interconnected. Or, we could say it this way: We participate in God's action through judgment and grace.

Often we experience God's activity first as judgment, but by this I don't mean the common understanding of judgment as fierce angry abuse. God's judgment comes to us as love—a love that desires that we be motivated only by God's presence, and that drives us to participate in the other places where love grows, places of shared vulnerability and weakness. God's judgment is not like that of the popular high school clique that seeks to tear others down to feel good about themselves. Rather, the judgment of God brings light to our barrenness, it reveals that we are weak and in need. It feels harsh only when our motives are shown to ingeniously hide our weaknesses. God calls us out from our hiding places and exposes our motives, but this is just the first step. It is from our weaknesses and yearning that we are invited to participate in the action of God. This is surely grace; it is grace that God chooses to find us at the places of our failure, brokenness, and emptiness. But not only does God find us in that place of weakness, God sweeps us up into God's own action, calling us to participate, through our weakness, in God's own ministry.

Consider the story of Moses. In his initial encounter with Yahweh, Moses is deeply aware that he is an elderly stuttering fugitive (Exodus 3). Invited to participate in God's saving act, Moses experiences this invitation as judgment, for the task is impossible for him. When we place our motives before the light and heat of the burning bush, we see that our motives are often self-centered, self-gratifying, or self-justifying, and that we often cloak these motives in religious garb like the Pharisees. We want kids to be good, to be servants, to be church members because we want to feel like we are making a difference, like our actions are significant and strong, like even if just one kid gets it, it is all worth it.

But those who are called into the action of God are forced to admit that their own actions are weak and pointless. Our actions outside the action of God are like a ninety-year-old man with a speech impediment who's been asked to topple the world's most powerful empire. The task before us is impossible. But from our impossibility, God moves. It is because of Moses' weakness that he is chosen. He is chosen to lead his people because his attempt to liberate his people through his own strength (by killing an Egyptian) had been shown to be bankrupt (Exodus 2). Now, eighty years old and a stuttering fugitive, he is ready to participate in the act of God. His judgment has become grace, for from his weakness he is sent to participate in the action of God.

What this means for me is that in ministry I participate in God's action not through my successes or accomplishments, but through my own death(s), through my honest admission that my motives too often are self-justifying and self-centered.

In honesty I live at the same time amid the judgment (death) and grace (love) of God. Therefore, the way I place my motive into the action of God is actually in the end no way at all. Or, to say it more correctly, it is the way of grace. For the way we participate in the act of God is to do as Moses and Sarah did: to admit that it is impossible, to articulate our weaknesses— *I'm an eighty-year-old man,* or *I'm unable to bear a child,* or *I have no idea what to do for young people,* or *My ambition always trips me up,* or *I doubt my faith more than I trust it.* When we admit our limits—when we confess that in our own power, we are powerless to do anything in ministry—that is when our own action is swept up into God's action. It is then that we do ministry from the location of grace, for God's action has judged us and, through our impossibilities, has made us alive. The doorway into the act of God is through God's judgment, through my brokenness and yearning. When I encounter God's act at this level, I realize that God's judgment *is* God's love, for God's very act is God's person. To participate in God's act is to participate in God's person, which calls each of us in love to live and minister from the depths of our own humanity.

When Nadia began contemplating what youth ministry was for, she felt exposed. Yet this wasn't a feeling of abusive vulnerability as much as a feeling of getting to the core, getting to the heart of her very self. As the light revealed the duplicity of her motives, she actually felt more human, more alive, more free. She began to realize that if youth ministry were for participating in the act of God, she could live into this only by being honestly human before and with young people, calling them into their own humanity, inviting them to contemplate and search for God in the barren empty spaces of their own lives.

It is only through this experience of judgment and grace that our motives and intentions come together. Those who are called to do youth ministry, those called to be proclaimers of the gospel, must do so from the place of their raw humanity, from their experience of broken dreams and deep regret. Love blooms from the manure of our raw humanity. It blooms from the judgment of God, which whispers, "I know you are weak. I know you are sad. But I am strong. Let me be your joy." It blooms from the judgment of God that says, "I will move—stop trying to do things on your own." It blooms from the judgment of God that tells us, "Stop trying to do youth ministry. I am the one who ministers through my love for young people. Follow me as I love young people, follow me through your own broken heart that yearns for love." And it is our hearing that judgment that leads to grace, allowing us to do ministry between judgment and grace.

When he encounters God in the burning bush, Moses takes God's action into his own by offering God his weakness, by admitting (confessing) to God that he is not able. God's love, like all love, reveals that we are in need, that we are weak—a weakness experienced not as humiliating exposure, but as nearness to the Beloved. When my wife picks up our daughter Maisy from school, Maisy's strong exterior often crumbles in seeing her mom. Bathed in Kara's love, Maisy is free to admit who she is, that she is weak, scared, or tired. Kara's love judges Maisy's self-protective exterior as untrue, and through the brokenness revealed by Kara's love, they embrace and share in each one's love for the other.

This is what I mean when I say that God's love is judgment. Moses realizes his brokenness and weakness in the heat of the burning bush. He is judged, but through this judgment

Moses is invited into God's action. Moses' weakness becomes the material for God's own action; the Israelites will know it is God who acts because Moses has no strength in and of himself. Moses goes to Egypt with the intention of freeing the people, but this is an intention born from a motive that has wrapped itself around his person, the motive given at the burning bush, the motive that is God's very person (God's very name) given in judgment and grace.

Moses will face the Pharaoh, motivated (empowered) by the burning bush, by the act of God. Like Abraham and Sarah who tried to act for God by commissioning Hagar as their surrogate, Moses had tried to free his people through his own action, the act of killing an Egyptian. But once Moses is judged as weak, God is ready to act, sending Moses back to the Pharaoh with one motive, not to liberate the people, but to participate in God's own action of liberating the people. Moses will warn the Pharaoh to let the people go or Yahweh will act again (and so Yahweh does with plagues and finally an exodus through a parted sea).

Soon after her conversation with Mrs. Davis, Nadia decided to stop trying to do youth ministry, to stop trying to be something. She decided that instead she would seek God—she would understand her vocation as a calling to participate in God's action with and for young people. But she soon realized that the only way she could do this was by living into her own deep questions. Therefore, she began to see herself not as a leader who tried to get young people to do something, but as a co-searcher, a companion who walked with young people as they sought for God next to their yearnings, as a guide who could invite young people into ministry through their emptiness. As she began to think this way, her very conception of who she was as a youth leader changed. She had over-looked Marty, now admitting to herself that it was because his brokenness seemed so obvious, in that he was overweight and quiet. But with her understanding of youth ministry as participation in the act of God, she saw Marty as having a deep ministry of his own, a ministry of seeking God in his questions and yearnings, of reaching out into the world as he followed the God who calls people from their brokenness to proclaim the gospel in word and deed.

Nadia was done trying to be a magician who could bring kids into the presence of God. Instead, she became a fellow yearner, seeking God alongside her young people. She saw her ministry as inviting kids to seek God from the places of their deep questions and open wounds; for the God who moves, the God who is active, is found bringing life out of barren places.

It is *not* that excellence, growth, and innovation are bad; in fact, they are to be desired. But these desires must be trans-formed, because excellence, growth, and innovation have a way of demanding the throne and becoming our sole motiva-tion. In short, they have a way of becoming idols. Excellence, growth, and innovation must be remolded in the heat of the burning bush. They, too, must be judged. What is excel-lent, growing, and worthy of innovation in youth ministry can only be that which draws us deeper into God's action, that which witnesses to an active God who touches us at our places of impossibility, making our impossibilities the vehicle for participation in God's own ministry.

And this was the heart of the conflict that Nadia felt with Mrs. Davis. At one level all Mrs. Davis wanted was for her daughter to feel entertained by the group. But this desire was given its gravitas by Mrs. Davis's intention that the youth ministry be excellent, growing, and innovative enough to hold her daughter's attention. When Nadia responded that it might be fine that her daughter finds the other youth ministry significant, Mrs. Davis was not satisfied. If Nadia's ministry were about excellence, then it would be conquering its competitors. But feeling herself stripped to the core of her humanity under the judgment of God, feeling embraced by God at the place of her deepest yearning, Nadia had a different vision of excellence, growth, and success. Instead of conquering competitors, this vision had something to do with searching for the core of each young person's own yearning humanity, seeking for God and God's action next to their searching. If the youth ministry across town was offering this to Mrs. Davis's daughter, fine. Nadia's concern was to seek for God in the humanity of the young people God placed in her care. Nadia contended that excellence, growth, and innovation were transformed when they were seen through the lens of the wandering and barrenness of young people, through the window of a God who sweeps wandering and barren people up into God's own action.

Nadia felt free. It was a freedom that she believed Chad had never felt; he had burnt out trying to magically get kids near God. Chad could never admit his own weakness, even when his weakness and fatigue were obvious to everyone else. Nadia felt like she could really be herself with young people, like the questions and confusion that both she and her kids had were not threats but invitations to seek God more deeply. She not only felt free but newly energized; she felt a new empowerment to go and seek God alongside these young people in this church and community, to seek God next to their concrete and beautiful humanity. She could feel her motivation and intentions coming together. Her motivation was simply to participate in God's action through her own brokenness; she intended to love and challenge young people to participate in God's action as a community by sharing deeply in one another's lives, by together seeking God next to their questions and yearnings. *That's my purpose!* she thought, as she picked up the phone to call Mrs. Davis. She looked forward to having an opportunity to share her new understanding, a time when she could tell Mrs. Davis why she wasn't concerned about entertainment but about inviting young people to contemplate a reality where God brings life from death.

MORE DRAMA

Several weeks after Nadia's lunch with Mrs. Davis, she found an email from Erica, the associate pastor, staring at her from her inbox. This was not uncommon: While Pastor Jerry was known for barging into your office, Erica was known for her emails. So when she first saw the message, Nadia thought little of it, figuring it was another of Erica's mass emails about something. But to Nadia's surprise it was a personal email addressed only to her.

It seemed that Erica had also been talking with Mrs. Davis—and not just Mrs. Davis but also some others from the group of church members who wanted the youth ministry to reach out into the community. Mrs. Davis had told Erica that her conversation with Nadia had been interesting and thought-provoking. In fact, Mrs. Davis had even called it "theologically insightful." Erica found this both shocking and intriguing, because she'd always considered youth ministry the least theological part of the entire church. Erica asked Nadia flat out in her email, "Do you imagine that you are doing something theological in the youth group? What I mean is: Are you doing something explicitly theological? What doctrines are you examining? How is theology answering kids' questions and confronting their problems? Are you using the creeds?" Erica concluded the email by stating, "I just find it so interesting (and honestly, weird) that you're using theology in youth ministry."

Contemplating Erica's questions about doctrines, answers, and creeds, Nadia now began to wonder if she really was doing theology. *What is theology, anyway?* She clearly wasn't doing theology the way Erica imagined. Nevertheless, she believed she was doing something theologically significant. Nadia knew she needed and wanted to respond to Erica, but she felt like they were working from completely different understandings of theology, and she had no idea how to begin to bridge the gap.

chapter four

How Youth Ministry Does Theology

Erica's email sat in Nadia's inbox for days. Nadia wanted to respond but remained unsure about what to say or how to say it. She began writing a few times, but deleted the email after just a few lines. Nadia was confident she was doing something theological, but then she would think to herself, *I don't even really know what theology is! I mean I don't really know how to define it.* Nadia knew that Erica often preached about doctrines and spoke often of the creeds. Erica loved quoting theologians that neither Nadia nor anyone else in the church had ever heard of. Nadia was fairly certain her work with the youth wasn't theological in the way Erica understood theology—which was probably why Erica had written her in the first place.

Nadia sat in front of her computer, staring at a blank email, tapping her fingers on her desk as if to awaken her mind. She thought about the seminary classes she'd taken, searching her brain to see if any of their content could now help her. She remembered parts of the intro lecture in her theology class, but it seemed irrelevant. All she recalled was her professor's discussing how theology had become an academic discipline; he never said anything about how it matters in ministry. She remembered sitting in the seminary cafeteria listening to students passive-aggressively belittling others for liking ministry classes more than systematic theology classes—as if the two could be so simply disconnected.

Those seminary experiences had given Nadia a bad taste for theology. And now Erica's questions had reminded her of its bitterness. But, unlike in seminary, this time Nadia wasn't willing to skip out on theology. She had discovered that youth ministry was for participation in God's action. This was both profoundly theological and too rich to be ignored. She needed to discover what theology was and how it worked as a way to participate in God's action.

As we move into this conversation about theology, it's important to acknowledge one fact: God is *not* a theologian. Theologians are important (and I count myself as one), but God never uses *theologian* as a self-description. As a matter of fact, none of the great players in the biblical narrative would define themselves primarily as theologians.[2] If there are theologians in the Bible, they're the Pharisees and Sadducees. God is not a theologian but a minister; God acts for the sake of making Godself known to the world. God acts so that creation might be reconciled to God, that all might live in the redemptive love of God. To say that God is active in the

---

2. Paul no doubt was a theologian, but my guess is that he would first define himself as a missionary—as one who spreads the word to the Gentiles. It is because of his ministry that Paul does theology, explaining why the Gentiles are included in God's new action through Jesus.

world (and that ministry is for participation in God's action) is to assert that God is ministering to the world. Everything we know about God is knowledge that flows out of God's actions. Theology at its most basic (and its most profound) is passionate reflection on God's action, on God's own ministry. This means *ministry actually makes theology possible.* Theology is the servant of ministry, because theology is reflection on God's action of ministry—which is often experienced in and through our own ministries, and in and through the ministry of the church. (This is why Karl Barth named his mammoth theological project *Church Dogmatics.*) To say it again, ministry makes theology possible—not the other way around, as Nadia so often experienced in the seminary cafeteria.[3]

This means (as we said at the beginning of the last chapter) that youth ministry is theological. But it isn't theological because it uses footnotes and big words; *youth ministry is theological because its very purpose is to participate in the action of God.* To think, feel, and partake in God's activity— this is to do theology, because it is to reflect deeply on who God is next to the lives and questions of young people. Once this becomes our purpose, once youth ministry is primarily about partnering with God in God's own actions with and for young people, then those who participate in ministry are thrust into theology. They are forced, like Moses, to ask why

---

3. Ray Anderson and Douglas John Hall agree when they say, "The 'practice,' of ministry, then, is not only the appropriate context for doing theological thinking, it is itself intrinsically a theological activity." "A Theology for Ministry," in *Theological Foundations for Ministry.* Ed. Anderson, Ray. (Edinburgh: T & T Clark, 1979), 7. In a later book, Hall writes, "Theology lives between the stories—God's story of the world, and humanity's ever-changing account of itself and all things. Theology is what happens when the two stories meet." *Thinking the Faith* (Minneapolis: Fortress , 1991), 91.

the bush burns but is not consumed. God's activity makes us into theologians, for in participating with God we are drawn into contemplation and reflection about who God is and what God is up to. But at the same time, God's activity also makes us into ministers, for God calls us not only to contemplate who this God of action is, but also to participate with God in God's action. The very fact that youth ministry is *ministry* means that it is theological—for it seeks to walk with young people as they encounter the God of the burning bush.[4]

CONTEXT AND CONTENT

When we make the assertion that ministry makes theology possible, we assert that God's action is both the context for ministry and the content of theology. Theology began mattering to Nadia because she saw that the context of ministering to young people was also the raw material (the content) for thinking about God, for doing theology. Nadia wanted nothing to do with the kind of theology that's done primarily in libraries. But the kind of theology she found apprehending her was a theology done in ministry, among people, next to the God who was acting in their midst. It was a theology that drew her into ministry through her own weakness and her need for a God who loved her from God's own being. Theology became intimate contemplation of young people, self, and God—it became *alive*. Theology became reflection on the living God, a God who is found in the brokenness and yearnings

---

4. "What is theology? It is neither mere repetition of church doctrines nor grandiose system-building. It is faith asking questions, seeking understanding. It is disciplined yet bold reflection on Christian faith in the God of the gospel." Daniel Migliore, *Faith Seeking Understanding: An Introduction to Christian Theology* (Grand Rapids, MI: Eerdmans, 2004), 19.

of young people. The very content of this theology (you could even say the starting point of theology) was the lives of this community of young people she'd been called to work with. Theology began for Nadia in the action of ministry; it was her calling as a minister that made her a theologian.

From this perspective, context and content were no longer divided as so often occurs in the realms of both theology and ministry. Instead, context and content were united. And in this fusion of context and content, Nadia felt not the boredom she had too often experienced in the seminary classroom but new energy—new energy to encounter young people, new energy to think big thoughts, even new energy to read the work of other theologians. Nadia realized that doing ministry in the context of God's activity is to be thrust into theological content.

Almost all of the theological content in the Old Testament begins with context. In witnessing God's liberating activity, in participating in God's action of redemption, the Israelites are given content for theology. The God who has redeemed is the same God who has created. Given that the Israelites have experienced redemption from slavery in Egypt, it is no wonder that redemption itself becomes the theological theme of the Hebrew Scriptures' account of creation: The God who redeems Israel from Egypt is the God who redeems creation from the chaos of nonbeing.

The God who encounters the Hebrews throughout the Old Testament is always placed in a context that is relational. This is the God of Abraham, Isaac, and Jacob; it is the God who is in ministry. There are never any assertions like "this is the God who is omnipotent," or "this is the God of transcendental metaphysics." Rather it is always within the context of

God's ministry with concrete people in time and space that we discover the content of who God is and what this God does: "I am the God of your fathers!" (Exodus 3:6). This God is a God who acts—and it is through the context of God's action that we discover the content of God's character.

When Nadia wrestled with the question "What is youth ministry for?" she found that youth ministry isn't about keeping kids good, making kids into something, or keeping them involved in a particular church tradition. Instead, ministry is about participating in God's act. And if this is true, then theology—understood as reflection on the action of God—is essential for ministry. When Nadia sees her purpose in ministry as participating in God's action, she becomes a theologian, for she must now seek to discern God's action within her own life and the lives of the young people to whom she's been called. She must reflect on the very nature and character of this God who is moving in their ministry, bringing life from death, and calling to them from a bush that burns but is not consumed.

YOUTH MINISTRY AND THEOLOGY

Youth ministry has often been criticized for lacking theological depth. Erica has long agreed with this critique. But this perception is *not* because youth ministry has been too fixated on ministry; rather, it's because youth ministry has often failed to reflect deeply on God's own ministry, on God's action with and for young people. Youth ministry, as it has become more professional and academic, has even given a great deal of attention to how a youth pastor or volunteer should act in ministry. But because it has not given the same attention to understanding God's action, it has lacked theological depth, justifying its action through bullet-pointed Bible verses or discussions of social-scientific literature regarding adolescent development, as opposed to seeking the mystery of the burning bush. Youth ministry has too often concerned itself with games, ministry models, and organizational charts rather than the very mystery of God's action in the world.

But theology begins with the burning bush that is never consumed (Exodus 3:2). It begins with the God who has heard the suffering and groaning of the people and who is ready to act. And this God calls Moses not to read a thesis or present an argument but to participate with God in God's action. Moses' story takes a theological turn when Moses asks for God's name (Exodus 3:14), when he seeks to understand who it is that is calling him into ministry and whose actions he will be following. God's response is as mysterious as the reality of the flaming bush that is not being consumed, "I am who I am" (Exodus 3:14). I am the one who moves. I am the one who encounters you!

This encounter at the burning bush and the exodus it leads to is often understood as Israel's central theological text. God's action to liberate them is central to their very identity as a people and to their understanding of the One who has freed them. It is from the tradition of Moses that the Torah (the first five books of the Hebrew Scriptures) would be written in the first place—recording the oral tradition of the creation narrative, the experience of the exodus, and the lives of patriarchs. Moses is no academic theologian but someone who is reflecting deeply on God's act in the context of ministry.

As I've reflected on this God of the burning bush, I've found four ideas that point toward doing theology as ministry. I believe each of them has direct relevance for youth ministry.

1. Action over Frozen Doctrine

We youth workers often view theology as a collection of doctrines we must get kids to understand and believe, rather than a way of thinking that draws us deeper into ministry. We see theology not as the process of thinking that connects our action with God's, but as the doctrinal seat belt, the safeguard that keeps our ministry from dangerous errors. Yet, if we're honest, we know teenagers' hearts are rarely set ablaze by the heat of doctrine; doctrines are too stilted, too linear, and often too cold to light a fire in a fifteen-year-old's heart. But at its core, theology is not doctrine; it is reflection on the action of a God who encounters dead and impossible realities for the sake of life. Doctrine is necessary and important, but it is not primary. The action of God—in our lives and in Scripture—is primary. Doctrine is to serve God's action.[5] What makes one a theologian in youth ministry is not her ability to repeat doctrines but her ability to notice and speak to God's presence in the context of the lives of her young people.[6]

Yet because theology is often equated with doctrine, we might be asked, "Does your ministry involve just hanging out with kids or do you get them into the Bible?" In other words: Are you about relationship or doctrine? There's an assumption that the two are opposed: You can either care deeply about being in relationship with kids and being involved in their lives, or you care about getting them to understand and believe the right doctrines. But from the location of the burn-

---

5. Scripture itself can become frozen when it is held captive by doctrine rather than understood as the Word of God. We will examine this in depth in book 3.

6. John Franke states, "The ultimate purpose of theology is not simply to establish 'right belief' but to assist the Christian community in its vocation to live as the people of God in the particular social-historical context in which it is situated." *The Character of Theology: An Introduction to Its Nature, Task, and Purpose* (Grand Rapids, MI: Baker, 2005), 161.

ing bush we see that action, God's action, precedes all doctrine, which means that our relationships may be the very place where the action of God is found, near the very cave where the bush burns brightly.

Moses is asked to take off his shoes because he is on holy ground (Exodus 3:5). But the ground is holy not because of doctrine, but because God is present. God is acting and, through the white-hot heat of God's fire, is transforming Moses' doctrines. Moses started the day wandering the hills with a conception (doctrine) that Elohim is one God—the God of Abraham, Isaac, and Jacob. But as he encounters the action of God in the burning bush, Moses' doctrine is melted into a new form. He comes to see that Elohim is Yahweh, that the God of his fathers is a God of redemption, a God who calls forth and sends forth, a God who speaks. And that, of course, is the point: Through the action of God, Moses is called to act—to go to Egypt and participate in God's work. The point of the encounter in the burning bush is not only to give Moses knowledge, but also to send Moses himself into action, into ministry. Too often biblical/doctrinally centered youth ministries are more about cognitive submission to doctrinal precepts than about participation—seeking to live into the profound reality where God moves.

It's a false choice to assume our youth ministries are either relational or doctrinal. Both relationships and doctrines must come under the judgment of God; they are both unhelpful if they avoid or attempt to supersede God's own action.[7] But if our focus is the action of God, then ministry becomes

---

7. "Christian theology is thoroughly relational throughout; and the relationship which is primary to it, i.e., the divine-human relationship, as well as the relationships which are conditioned by this primary relation (human to human, human to nature, etc.) honors the otherness of both partners." Hall, *Thinking The Faith*, 288.

essentially about encountering God in the lives of young people, about young people encountering the movement of God in their own lives as well as the lives of one another, adults, and the church community. And if this is our approach, then relationship and theology can't be divided.

Of course, there has been much conversation in the youth ministry world about how little young people actually know about the faith and how limited is their ability to articulate its central beliefs.[8] We've responded by adding more doctrine to our youth ministries, developing new models for helping kids comprehend and speak about their faith. But I wonder if the problem isn't so much that we've neglected doctrine (as a matter of fact, even churches that focus deeply on doctrine still scored low), but that we've failed to invite young people to open their lives to the act of God. We failed to invite them to seek the burning bush, which is found right next to the dark cave of our own wandering and weakness. To discover the act of God in this way is to find ourselves on holy ground, for the God found next to our wandering and weakness is a God who speaks.

For Erica, theology is primarily doctrine, but Nadia sees theology as something more, as participation through judgment and grace in the act of God. It is honestly exposing her deepest questions to God and seeking for God in them. Nadia is doing theology because she is seeking with young people to encounter God—a task that is complicated and rigorous. It's not that doctrine doesn't matter to Nadia; it does, but only as

---

8. See the National Study of Youth and Religion in Christian Smith and Melinda Lundquist Denton, *Soul Searching: The Religious and Spiritual Lives of American Teenagers* (Oxford: Oxford University Press, 2005).

guide or map that leads into deeper reflection on the God who is acting, the God who is found in the caves of young people's despair and broken hearts, the God whose healing love burns but is never consumed. Nadia is a theologian because she has placed action over doctrine, because she has invited young people to take off their shoes—for in the cave of their shared yearning, God is acting, the bush is burning.

2. Mystery over Frozen Knowledge

When we free theology from subordination to doctrine, when we make the action of God the content of theology, we are pushed into mystery. By focusing on the act of God, we make the assertion that what we see is not all there is, that there is more to reality than can be perceived. Young people already sense this in their being; they sense that to exist is more mysterious than rational, that there is more hidden within existence than we are able to know. When we see theology as simply imposing doctrine, we actually cut young people off from searching the mystery of their very existence. We worry that if they immerse themselves in the mystery for too long, then they will fall away from belief in pure doctrine.

But without the invitation to enter mystery, to think unthinkable thoughts, theology becomes stalled and meaningless. A theology without mystery is cut off from the dynamic action of God and settles for the idol of doctrinal knowledge. Action itself is mysterious—why anyone acts or does what he or she does is laced with mystery. It is a mystery why my wife loves me; it is all the more a mystery that God loves me and chooses to act within the world.

One of the greatest gifts young people give the church is their very imagination, which is the vehicle into mystery.

The church needs young people and all their questions to shake up those of us with mortgages and careers, to awaken us to big questions, to confront that what we can see is not all there is.

So often youth ministry sees its job as providing young people with knowledge that will solve their problems.[9] When kids struggle with Darwinian evolution at school, we provide knowledge-based apologetics of another perspective, battling one rationality with another. As young people confront the tension of the culture's sexual promiscuity, we provide knowledge on why "waiting" is a better option, why rationally it fits better with God's plan. But when we do this, we make these issues battles between competing sets of formal rationality, rather than inviting young people to confront these issues alongside mystery—a mystery that does not bend knee to formal rationality, where two things can exist as the same, where what is hidden and small may be more powerful than what is visible and prominent, and where what is true may at first glance seem absurd. We tend to think theology will provide us with the knowledge to solve young people's problems, rather than function as a very way of being and seeing the world, a way of searching for God in the world.

The danger with frozen knowledge is that it can stand in opposition to mystery. But the pillars of Christian faith are not built on the foundation of rational knowledge. Rather the pillars of Christianity rest on the cornerstone of the mystery

---

9. Daniel Migliore explains, "A mystery is very different from a problem. While a problem can be solved, a mystery is inexhaustible. A problem can be held at arm's length; a mystery encompasses us and will not let us keep a safe distance." *Faith Seeking Understanding*, 4.

of Jesus Christ (Romans 16:25), the mystery that God (*God!*) entered our world in Jesus, that the forsaken Galilean is the Lord, the fulfillment of God's kingdom—a kingdom only seen with eyes that look into mystery.

Moses is drawn to the bush because it is a mystery: How can it burn yet never be consumed? Rationally, all that burns is consumed, but not here. An irrational mystery is before Moses; his imagination moves him deeper into the cave to investigate further what he is seeing. When God speaks, it remains a mystery. God will not so easily be apprehended; God is not a thing to possess, but an Other who invites us into relationship. When Moses asks for God's name, he is told that God is "I AM" (Exodus 3:14)—an answer that reveals who God is, yet only deepens the mystery. Moses learns that to participate with God is to open oneself to mystery.[10]

One Wednesday night Nadia asked the kids to bring with them some kind of artifact that caused them to think more deeply about their own lives. She told them it could be a song, a movie clip, a poem, a picture—anything that moved them into thinking deeply about mystery, about the mystery of their existence, the mystery of the question, *What is a lifetime and why do we live it?* Nadia was shocked by the things kids brought, but even more shocked at the questions they were confronting. Beth shared Anna Nalick's song "Breathe," focusing on one particular line: "And life's like an hourglass glued to the table." Beth explained, "I don't really even like

---

10. Karl Barth says it this way: "Theology means rational wrestling with the mystery. But all rational wrestling with this mystery, the more serious it is, can lead only to its fresh and authentic interpretation and manifestation as a mystery." *Church Dogmatics* I.I. (Edinburgh: T & T Clark, 1936), 368.

this song, but when I hear this line, I wonder about how short my life is and how, like, I can never get some experiences back, and it makes me wonder why God makes life so short."

After every kid shared about the items they'd brought and the questions the items raised, Nadia announced that it was time to contemplate this theologically. She read aloud the story of Moses' encounter with God at the burning bush and then asked: *"Who is this God, and what is this God doing? How is this God found within our questions?"* Nadia was amazed by how this ignited their imaginations. She was shocked by the sometimes profound, sometimes crazy theological assertions they came up with. But she was convinced that they were *doing* theology, contemplating the very mystery of existence, an existence where the God who is "I am" is found.

3. Issues over Frozen Principles

At its heart, all theology is practical. Theology is to assist the people of God in participating in the action and mystery of God. This means that good theology, although it dwells in mystery, cannot be abstract. It cannot be a collection of principles with no real connection to our lives. Theology may call us to think big thoughts, but these big thoughts are embedded in our very lives. As we've said, we know God through God's own action, and God's action is found in the stories of our lives and the lives of the people of God throughout history. This means theology is more about issues than principles; it is about confronting the realities we face rather than a static set of principles. The Bible isn't a book of principles, but a narrative of the people of God encountering God through the issues they confront (such as slavery, interaction with other peoples, and exile).

Moses is beckoned to the burning bush because of an issue—his people's oppression. God has heard their groaning (Exodus 6:5). Moses isn't called to the burning bush to receive theological principles, but to participate in God's action—and God's action moves within the concrete situations of our lives. Even the Ten Commandments aren't principles in a formal sense; they are ways of acting in accord with the being and acting of God. They are not frozen principles that can be disconnected from the action of God in the issues of our lives. The Ten Commandments are relevant, life-giving, and empowering only to those who have seen the hand of God's freedom, to those who have participated in the action of God amid the issues of their lives. Of course, that hasn't stopped people from trying to disconnect the commandments from God's action. Jesus rebuked the Pharisees because they had made the Law into a set of principles disconnected from the action of God. Keeping the Sabbath, for example, became a principle that was no longer connected to God's own action (Mark 2:27). But when understood in proper context, the Ten Commandments are ways of living in relationship with the very action of God.[11]

We youth workers tend to be addicted to principles: principles that will make our ministries more successful, principles that will rejuvenate our spiritual lives. And we pass principles

---

11. "When the Jewish people later took the Commandments out of this living relation to a redeeming God and made of them an abstract rule of righteousness, they destroyed this inner logic. The commandment of the Sabbath, for example, became a formal principle with absolute authority. Permitting no exception." Ray S. Anderson, *The Soul of Ministry* (Louisville: Westminster John Knox, 1997), 20.

onto others, like giving parents principles that can help them parent more effectively, or giving kids principles to guide them in sharing their faith. That's all fine. But all these principles can easily lead us to think theology is about accumulating and mastering principles.

But when it comes to theology, principles do a strange thing. Principles put the onus for action on us, placing the focus on what *we* do rather than what God does with and for us. Principles also have a way of calling our obedience to them, rather than to the God that moves in history. Principles can be like a black hole that pulls all our action into it; we end up doing everything we can to live up to and enact our principles. In the process, they only allow room for one application, thus minimizing and oversimplifying the issues we are really facing.[12] Principles tend to consider context irrelevant; their great value is that they can be applied to anyone's life or situation without much adaptation. But principle-centered ministry and theology tend to ignore the deep issues we face for the sake of mastering the principle.

Yet, a theology that seeks to reflect on the act of God—and a youth ministry that seeks to participate in the action of God—sees issues as more central than principles. The specific issues our young people face become the textbook for theological reflection. Their issues (my mom has cancer; I hate my body; I'm lonely and don't know how to make friends) provide the very shape of theological reflection. They become doorways into seeking for God as we reflect on who God is and what God is doing next to these very issues that spring from the hearts of young people.

---

12. Thanks to Eric Leafblad for conversation on this point.

Every time Nadia planned a Bible study, Sunday school lesson, or talk, she took time to reflect deeply about the issues the kids in her group were facing. Nadia always started their conversations by placing issues at the center of their attention. Reflecting on the real struggles they were facing gave them new eyes to see the biblical text or lesson; it gave them theological insight that touched the very heart of their existence.[13]

4. Questions over Answers

When Nadia started in youth ministry, she thought a big part of her job was to answer all the questions kids had about faith and God. She found this daunting—but figured sooner or later she'd be able to do this. She thought if she could just read the right books and complete that seminary education she'd be able to answer most of kids' questions. But that presumes that most of kids' questions could be answered, and answered by doctrine and principles. Nadia always felt she was in a rush to find the resources that would allow her to answer kids' questions. In fact, that's why she found seminary so annoying; she always felt herself saying under her breath, "Just give me the answer already!"

But once Nadia saw youth ministry as participation in God's action, she began to realize her job wasn't to be a dispenser of answers. Maybe her more important role was to become the one who encouraged young people to ask questions for themselves. This was not so she could provide easy

---

13. Hall says it this way: "Theology is a spiritual discipline in the sense that it assumes the stance of listener, not only to the various tangible sources that we have described in the preceding sections, but also to an intangible, transcendent, but nonetheless present reality named by our tradition *Spiritus Sanctus*." *Thinking the Faith*, 283.

answers, but rather as a way of inviting them to dwell on the action of God in their lives, as a way into mystery.[14]

Moses has direct questions for the God revealed in the burning bush, but he is given no clear answers. He's told that the truth he seeks is found in following the One who encounters him, following the One who acts. In response to his questions, Moses is told to go back to Egypt; his questions will be answered through participation with God in God's action. Yahweh leaves many of Moses' questions unanswered because those questions, his searching and yearning, are doorways into participation with God, for searching and yearning is where theology and ministry, context and content, come together. There is no answer to why the bush burns but is not consumed. There is only the realization that it is God who encounters Moses. And that his participation in the question is more important than any answer he might find.

As she wrote to Erica, Nadia finally found her fingers typing quickly. Finally, she was stringing sentences into paragraphs. She expressed her appreciation for Erica's theological mind, admitting that she would never have a handle on doctrine and systematic arguments the way Erica did. But Nadia

---

14. Migliore writes, "As long as Christians remain pilgrims of faith, they will continue to raise questions—hard questions—for which they will not always find answers. Rather than having all the answers, believers often find that they have a new set of questions. This is surely the experience of the women and men in the Bible. The Bible is no easy answer book, although it is sometimes read that way. If we are ready to listen, the Bible has the power to shake us violently with its terrible questions: 'Adam, where are you?' (Gen. 3:9). 'Cain, where is your brother Abel?' (Gen. 4:9). To judge the cause of the poor and needy—'Is not this to know me? says the Lord' (Jer. 22:16). 'Who do you say that I am?' (Mark 8:29). 'My God, my God, why have you forsaken me?' (Mark 15:34). When faith no longer frees people to ask hard questions, it becomes inhuman and dangerous." *Faith Seeking Understanding*, 6.

went on to explain that, for her, theology was more active than static, more about seeking God in the issues of our lives than in books and intellectual arguments. Theology was the invitation to participate with God in a new reality, in the mystery of God's own activity in the world—at least that's what Nadia was trying to say. Nadia pushed to explain that she saw theology primarily as practical, as a way of "faith seeking understanding" next to our deepest yearnings. Nadia admitted she had much to learn, but explained that she was seeking to make young people's lives the primary text of theological reflection—because youth ministry was about participation in God's own action with and alongside those young people.

As she moved her cursor over the "send" button, Nadia held her breath. Then she took one last quick inhale and clicked. It was off, and her outbox was now empty.

A few hours later, Erica responded. Seeing Erica's message sitting in her inbox, Nadia said to herself, "Here we go," assuming Erica would judge her thinking to be at best misdirected—if not downright heretical. But Nadia's anxiety was unnecessary. Erica's response was positive and affirming; she even said, "I think this is harder than knowing all the arguments and doctrines, and takes a real, deeply thinking theologian." Then Erica offered, "How about we commit to meet with each other? Maybe I can help you reflect on some doctrines and concepts, and you can help me be a theologian who seeks for God in the context of our lives." For the first time, Nadia felt like Erica truly saw her as an equal—not just as the one who worked with kids, but as a fellow minister of the gospel who was seeking to do something deeply theological.

THE DRAMA

The very next day, Nadia had breakfast with one of the parents in her church. Evan was in his late thirties and was married with two kids. He'd been a youth worker "back in the day," as he would say. After college he worked his way through seminary as a youth pastor, before finishing his MA in ethics and taking a position at a denominational publishing company. Evan had been one of the central figures in Nadia's interview process. He was among the group of elders and other congregation members who wanted to see the youth ministry be about outreach, helping kids from the community come to faith. If Mrs. Davis's wanting the youth ministry to be fun for the kids of the church represented one camp, Evan was in the other. As he said many times in Nadia's interview, "Youth ministry is all about evangelism."

Evan had called a week ago, offering to take Nadia out for breakfast. Nadia knew that for her that breakfast would be more about listening than talking. Evan was always filled with ideas and eager to share them, making it hard for Nadia (or anyone else who spoke with him) to find space to squeeze in a comment.

The breakfast went as Nadia expected. Evan talked about his family, the church, and his passion for outreach in youth ministry. Nadia just listened intently, hypnotically enjoying the energy Evan expressed.

But then, like the sudden halt of a downpour on a humid summer day, Evan stopped talking. The silence pierced Nadia's ears. She quickly realized he'd stopped because he was awaiting her answer. He had finished his downpour of verbiage with a question that only now registered in Nadia's mind, "So what do you think ministry is? I've heard you say that youth ministry is *ministry* because it participates in God's own action. But what then is ministry? I mean, ministry is something you *do,* right? Ministry is something that I think I do—I mean, I'm really excited about being a lay minister. But honestly, when you start talking about God's ministry, and how we should be participating in God's ministry, I lose what ministry is. So . . ."

Pausing to rewind her mind to mentally grab hold of the question, Nadia started to answer, but as she did, she realized the depth and significance of the question. "Well . . ." she said, pausing again, "Well . . ." and she launched in.

chapter five

What is
Ministry, Really?

Nadia believed that her work was at its core *ministry*, meaning it was participation in God's own action. But now Evan confronted her with how this understanding of ministry connected with what she actually did. How did her actions in ministry connect with God's action? Nadia knew that youth ministry was theological because youth ministry wrestled with the action of God in young people's lives. But if God's action was to minister to creation and bring us back into relationship with God, what was her ministry? Nadia wondered if her theological musing had eliminated the need for her job. What was her ministry next to the ministry of God? God's ministry with Abraham and Sarah was to bring about a people, with Moses to bring forth exodus, all for the purpose of bringing reconciliation (new relationship) to humanity. How was Nadia participating in this same ministry?

Six months ago if you'd asked Nadia, "What is ministry?" she would have provided you with a list of things people in ministry do. She would have begun answering this question by mentally reviewing her calendar. But now she couldn't do that. She knew that what those in ministry did was participate in God's ministry (and this is what made them theologians). But now Evan's question forced her to have to confront another question, "What is God's ministry and how do we participate in it?" She had never seen this before. It wasn't enough to just see youth ministry as participation in God's own ministry, but now she had to explore what God's ministry is in the world.

Evan remained quiet, something unusual for him. He looked intensely at her as if really wanting to enter a conversation. So Nadia began thinking out loud with Evan. "Well," she said, "when I think of ministry theologically, I think of God's action to enter . . ."

"Right," Evan interrupted, "right, ministry is all about mission, God is on a mission, and so are we. Ministry equals mission. And I think . . ." As the verbal downpour resumed, Nadia just stared back, mouth open, feeling as if her words had been scraped from her tongue and thrown in a bin labeled "uninterested." Nadia just sat there in that uncomfortable place of having your thoughts move from your head to your mouth, but then finding no one is listening. In this state, Nadia found herself exposed to Evan's verbal storm; she felt herself bare to the harsh weather of his insensate talking.

MISSION AND GOSPEL

After her meeting with Evan, Nadia felt more stuck than ever before. She felt caught between the expectations of these two groups represented by Evan and Mrs. Davis. Nadia had felt like she'd had a breakthrough with Mrs. Davis; Mrs. Davis seemed to understand Nadia's perspective of youth ministry as participation in God's action. But as they'd concluded their conversation, Mrs. Davis said words that still touched Nadia. With wide, teary eyes, Mrs. Davis said, "I guess, all I really want, even more than Amanda liking the youth group, is for her to experience the gospel. I want her to see it as good news. I want all the kids in the church to understand the gospel." And now, even as Mrs. Davis's moving confession pulled Nadia's heart in one direction, Evan's monolithic passion for mission was tugging at her every limb. And it wasn't that she didn't agree with Evan or Mrs. Davis. It was just that she felt the crushing pressure of their perspectives; she felt squeezed between gospel and mission.

When answering the question, "What is ministry?" we find ourselves thinking about gospel and mission. But too often we've assumed gospel and mission to be two very different, if not opposing, realities. Maybe we think that the goal of mission is to give people the gospel. A missionary, after all, goes to a new place with the mission of spreading the gospel. Therefore, mission is one thing and gospel is another. The conversations with Evan and Mrs. Davis made Nadia feel as if she were stuck between the two. Each of the groups they represented seemed to assume Nadia needed to choose one or the other, that she could make the youth ministry either about kids growing in understanding of the faith (gospel) or about outreach to others (mission).

But this is not an either/or equation. Gospel and mission are not two poles that should be understood in opposition to each other. Rather, gospel and mission are two sides of the same coin. They are fundamentally interconnected; neither can exist without the other. There is no gospel without mission, and there is no mission without gospel. The gospel is the good news of God's action, the articulation of the truth that in the midst of the reality of death, God has acted for our salvation, overcoming death with life. Mission is how we *participate* in this reality, recognizing that this God who overcomes death with life is moving in the world, confronting death with life. The good news, the gospel, is that this God is active in ministry, on a mission to overcome death with life.[15]

The good news of the gospel *is* God's mission, and God's mission is the good news of the gospel. God is moving and active. The God who heard the groaning of the Israelites in Egypt and acted (in mission) to liberate them is still acting today. This is the good news. Gospel and mission can only be separated when we detach them from the act of God. And this detachment occurs most often when our focus turns from God's action to our own. In divine action, mission and gospel are inseparable; only in human action can we choose either to teach the gospel or to do missional outreach.

In God's action then, gospel and mission exist together, for the gospel is God's very self coming to us, meeting us in our places of death and overcoming death with life. The church that reaches out in mission is the church that has come to understand the gospel as God's very ministry to them. We have the gospel, the good news, because God has moved, because God has heard our groaning and acted with and for us. This means gospel and mission can never be separated. Mrs. Davis and Evan are misguided to assume that the youth ministry must be devoted to just one or the other. Rather, if youth ministry participates in the action of God, then it sees gospel and mission as

---

15. Karl Barth says it like this, "The One who in revelation calls us out of our enmity against Him to Himself, who calls us out of death into life, is the One who in so doing also makes Himself known as the One who previously called us out of nothing into existence, into existence as pardoned sinners, yet into existence as pardoned sinners." *Church Dogmatics* I.1, 444.

inseparable. It sees itself living in the proclamation of the gospel as God's action, God's mission to overcome death with life.

Evan had conflated mission with human action. What he wanted was *not* for the youth ministry to participate in God's activity with and among the young people in the community. Evan wanted Nadia to do missional and evangelistic *things*. Though he knew better intellectually, he functioned as if he believed mission is about what *we* do, as opposed to how God acts in the world.

Youth ministry has no shortage of events, resources, and tools to help youth workers who want to do missional or evangelistic outreach or deepen kids' knowledge and understanding of the gospel. Every youth ministry convention is saturated with flyers advertising such things. But almost all these events and resources focus on human action, on what we should do, how we might reach or covert or motivate young people. By focusing on human action they tend to divide gospel and mission. And one result is that the gospel we communicate has little to do with a God who is active in mission, seeking to take all that is dead and make it alive. This God is static—little more than a stagnant pool of knowledge—and the techniques and resources are all about getting kids to accept the right collection of facts about God. It's no wonder many of them find our God and our religion stale. Our words sound hollow and taste dry and lifeless because our God has become an idol, a being we are devoted to but who is unable to move, act, or speak (Acts 17:16–34). The God we present is not the God of the burning bush that in mystery and wonder is never consumed. We don't talk about the God who is, then and now, on a mission, calling out and moving Moses to encounter God's own person and then become a part of God's liberating activity.

Moses encounters a God who acts (and speaks)—and this

action of God becomes the gospel. It saves Moses from his state as fugitive wanderer; it promises to save the Israelites. But it is the gospel because this is God who moves, who is on the move, calling Moses to join Yahweh in the mission of liberating God's people. The mission of liberation becomes the gospel, the good news to Israel, the good news that would be the nation's most defining story. In the burning bush there is no separation between gospel and mission, because gospel and mission are united in the character and action of Godself.

It is God's action that holds gospel and mission together, because in the end the gospel is God's very heart, and mission is God's very desire to be with and for us from the heart of God's love for us. This means that mission (or evangelism) in youth ministry is about participation in God's action of bringing life out of death. We don't set up "midnight madness" events for our kids as a way of breaking down their walls so they are more susceptible to the message of the gospel. Rather, as participants in the gospel, we hold midnight madness outreach events in order to encounter young people, to seek for the action of God next to their lives, to witness to the gospel through our care for them. On the night of the event, instead of saying, "Hey, kids, the reason we did all this is so we could tell you about Jesus," we say, "Hey, kids, we did all this because we want to know you, because we think you're important, and we think this because we've experienced God's action in our lives, and God's action opens our eyes to see you and want to be with you. So we invite you to walk with us as we seek for this God."

REVELATION

In God's freedom God chooses to make Godself known. We can encounter God only because God chooses to reveal Godself through God's action. Scripture declares that no one can see God and live (Exodus 33:20), yet God walks with Adam, God addresses Abraham, and God sends Moses. God has broken into the world and made Godself known to us (John 1). The knowledge we have about who God is comes from God's action of unveiling Godself. Theology is born from revelation. This is what makes theology living, because it seeks to reflect not on the ruminations in dusty old library books but on the action of the living God to make Godself known in the world.[16]

But it is not only theology that finds its source in revelation. In the same way, ministry finds its source in revelation. When, where, and how God reveals Godself is the *content* of theology. But this content demands that we also give attention to *context*, because this God reveals Godself in history and in our lives. Therefore, theology and ministry become fused, because to gain knowledge of God's revelation is to experience God's ministry—which is the very giving of Godself in God's revelation. But, again, this sounds like a whole lot of theological jargon. What does it actually mean?

Nadia had responded to Evan's question about the nature of God's mission by stating, "I think God's mission is God's acting to reveal God's very self to us. God's mission is to reveal Godself to us by encountering us, overcoming death and sin by acting to give us God's very self."

"I don't see that as very missional," Evan responded.

"No, no, it really is," said Nadia, shifting in her seat, as if the energy of her thoughts made her wiggle. "It is, because God's very mission is to give us Godself: to give us life, justice,

---

16. Karl Barth says, "All revelation, then, must be thought of as revealing, i.e., as conditioned by the act of revelation." *Church Dogmatics* I.1, 119.

and mercy in God's own person. God's mission is to free us from the death of sin and oppression. Mission is the gospel." Evan just stared back, so Nadia continued, "What I mean is, God's mission is God revealing Godself, and we (whether it's you, or me, or the youth group) participate in it." But she realized that Evan was neither following her nor seemed interested.

That evening, Nadia found herself reliving the conversation on the ride home, continuing to grind on her theological breakthrough. As she did, she said to herself, "But the question becomes where and to whom does God reveals Godself? In other words, how is God revealed?"

Nadia had a number of friends in college who talked constantly about how they saw God acting in their daily lives. God was calling them to do all kinds of things and providing them with everything from parking spots to good dates to the wisdom to find a great sale on jeans. God was the noun of active verbs, sure—but there was really no substance to this thinking. God was talked about constantly, but never reflected on enough to qualify the talk as theology; it lacked any precision in articulating how God acts. Nadia wanted to avoid these kinds of simplistic conceptions of how God moves in our world. She understood God's action to mean much more than providing parking spaces, boyfriends, and sales on jeans.

When we seriously contemplate God's act of revelation (and throughout the next three books in this series we'll explore more fully how to contemplate God's revelation), we know we can't settle for easy ideas about how God works in our world. God's action is the revealing of God's very being, a being that encounters us in judgment, in our impossibility, our bareness, our exile, our death, giving us the sure grace of new life. God's revelation in sending Moses to Egypt strikes Moses as deep judgment. Moses' weakness becomes lit by the burning bush. God calls Moses into God's person by sending him into God's mission. While this is first experienced as judgment, it also becomes grace, for God reveals that it will be out of Moses' own impossibilities, the very impossibilities of the people Moses is sent to, that God will act. God will act by revealing Godself as Yahweh, giving the people God's very name, saving them (the gospel) by revealing God's very person to them.

Youth ministry has tended to see knowledge of God not as an encounter with the very revelation of God, with the very revealing of Godself in our lives, but as a stagnant pool of facts that we hope young people will assimilate and accept. This is one reason we youth workers are often more interested in discussing human action ("A youth minister should do this!" Or, "Junior highers are like that . . .") than in seeking the unveiling of the God of the burning bush in young people's lives.[17]

And, when we *have* talked about the action of God, when we do call young people to seek for God in their lives, we've tended to sound like Nadia's college roommates. We've called them to look for God in moments of self-improvement, in experiences of luck, and in feelings of success. "What is God doing in your life?" asked at a high school Bible study leads to testimonies of B+ grades when I forgot to study, video games desired and gotten, and wins for sports teams.

Our talk of God's action can become flat and simplistic because we don't understand God's action as springing from

---

17. Douglas John Hall states, "Revelation is not, then, the communication of ideas about God and the things of God, even though ideas are included in the experience of revelation, as they are included in the experience of meeting another human being. Revelation, however, is the 'divine-human encounter' (Emil Brunner)." *Thinking the Faith,* 407.

God's revelation. God's revelation is the radical move of God to make Godself known, to be found in the world. Youth ministry has a hard time making the action of God the center of its purpose, holding together both gospel and mission, because youth ministry has not talked about the action of God in this way. We've settled instead for very abstract conceptions of how and where we encounter God—if you pray, if you feel something in worship, if something good happens to you. But the Christian confession is that God has acted to make Godself known. To do youth ministry from the place of contemplating God's revelation is to have something concrete to say to young people about who God is and where God is moving in the world.

When we ask young people what God is doing in their lives, we often fail to give them ways of discerning this theologically, other than assuming that God shares in their wants and optimistic hopes. A kids figures: God is good, wants me to be happy, and has some superpowers; therefore, I see God in those areas of my life where I get what I want—like my team winning or a good grade when I didn't work for it. After all, the kid figures, these experiences *could* be God, because if the kid had a superpower, he'd use it to get good grades without studying.

BACK TO MOSES

But this then leads us back to Moses and his encounter with God in the burning bush, and his experience of God as both judgment and grace. And it leads us not just to Moses but also to other key biblical moments in salvation history. It appears that God's revelation, God's act to reveal Godself, is often surrounded by despair, yearning, and brokenness from the human side. God is revealed in those moments when human action encounters impossibility. God's judgment is not harsh condemnation, but the articulation of what is; it is the reality of enslavement, barren wombs, stuttering prophets, insignificant nations, and pregnant girls living in the godforsaken Galilee.

God's revelation comes in hidden and backward ways—most ultimately being hidden and backward in the full humanity and full divinity of Jesus Christ. Moses is called to encounter God in the hiddenness of the dark cave; in ultimate backwardness Moses is called into the mission of God not through Moses' strength, but through his weakness. Mission and gospel are inseparable because God's mission is born out of the good news of God coming near and using our weaknesses, taking what is dead in us and using it to bring life not only to us but to creation.[18]

---

18. Daniel Migliore explains, "At the same time, for the New Testament witness as for the Old, the revelation of God is, paradoxically, a hidden revelation. The hiddenness of God in Jesus Christ is not simply that he is a finite, vulnerable, mortal creature like other human beings. Rather, God's self-discloser is hidden in the servant form of this person and above all in his crucifixion. As Paul recognizes, the message of God's act of revelation and reconciliation in a humble servant who suffers and is crucified for our sake is sheer scandal and folly to the wise and powerful of this world (1 Cor. 1:22-23)." He continues, "The theologians of the Eastern church emphasize the darkness of God, by which they mean the hiddenness and incomprehensibility of the essence of God. Thomas Aquinas frequently reminds us that God remains largely hidden to finite human reason: 'No created intellect can comprehend God wholly.' The theme of God's hiddenness is very prominent in Luther's theology: 'God has hidden himself in Christ.' According to Barth, all serious knowledge of God begins with the knowledge of the hiddenness of God, i.e., the inalienable freedom and surprising grace of God who is self-revealed in Jesus Christ. 'God's hiddenness . . . meets us in Christ, and finally and supremely in the crucified Christ; for where is God so hidden as here, and where is the possibility of offense so great as here?' Implicit or explicit in the many variations on the theme of the hiddenness of God in the Christian theological tradition is the confession that in Jesus Christ crucified and risen, God is truly revealed yet also, paradoxically, hidden." *Faith Seeking Understanding,* 25–26.

God chooses to unveil Godself in hiddenness and back-wardness because God's mission is the good news of God overcoming death with life. And the only way to overcome death without serving it is to bear death, to become weak and use backwardness, like old stuttering prophets and crosses rather than generals and weapons.

Too often in youth ministry we characterize the action of God (what is God doing in your life?) only in the realm of the obvious—my team won, I guess that was God; I still feel excited about my new jeans, I guess that was God, too. But usually God does not reveal Godself in the obvious, but in the hidden, in the opposite. Nadia was starting to see this; she was noticing that even though God is glory and power, the biblical narrative shows a God who chooses to come to us in weakness and suffering—most fully in the incarnate Christ (see 2 Cor-inthians). And this reality was helping her to seek for God's action in young people's lives not in the obvious (the joys and successes) but in the profound, the places where God took what was old and brought forth the new. This is why it takes the eyes of faith to see God's action; it takes faith to see the God of glory hidden amid our deepest yearnings and brokenness.

When we ask young people to discern the action of God, we ask them to reflect on the revelation of God and, in doing so, to reflect on their own yearning and brokenness. We ask them to search for God in those places where yearning and broken-ness are shared, where others join us, binding themselves to us not around but within our yearning and brokenness. This is what I have referred to in other books as *place-sharing.* Place-sharing seeks to be in relationship with young people as the location of God's very presence, because place-sharing seeks to conform itself to the very action of God. Yahweh is the God who is revealed when Yahweh hears the groaning of Yahweh's broken people.

EX NIHILO

God's revelation, God's action of unveiling, most often comes *ex nihilo*, it comes out of nothing. Its coming happens in a place, in a particular context, but its arrival is not dependent or contingent on that context. The church has often confessed that creation itself is *ex nihilo*, "out of nothingness." And this has something to say about where we should expect to encounter God's action. Now, it may very well be true that God provides parking spots, B-pluses, and bargain jeans. God may be pulling the strings on the insignificant things in the world—we would do well to allow for such a possibility. But this is not the place to seek for God's action, because such events have little to do with mission and gospel. From the very beginning, from creation, God has moved (acted) out of nothingness. So, even if God is pulling all the strings that lead to homecoming wins, cheap jeans, and surprise grades, these things are not the location for primarily encountering the God of the burning bush in ministry.

The God of the burning bush reveals Godself out of human impossibility. Sarah is ninety, Abraham is impotent, Moses is a stutterer, and David is too young and small to be considered. God reveals Godself next to nothingness and impossibility; the breaking in of God often happens next to human weakness and yearning, in the backward and hidden (1 Corinthians 1:18). It is here that God moves; it is here that God is revealed; it is here that gospel and mission are linked. God's mission is to enter our impossibilities with the goodness that from the act of God a new reality in the love of God is breaking forth.[19]

So when we ask young people, "What is God up to in your life, where is God moving?" we are compelled to look for God's action in the kinds of places where God is revealed. We look for God in places of brokenness, yearning, and suffering, places where God takes these deaths upon Godself for the sake of life. God is active at the places of our raw humanity. It is here, in our raw humanity, that we enter gospel and mission, that gospel and mission are held together. For the God of creation, the God who hears the groaning of God's people, acts where there is the scent of nothingness. The God of exodus acts in those places where we are held captive, revealing Godself so death might be overcome with life.

RECONCILIATION

But this then leads us to something even deeper. Whenever God reveals Godself, there is reconciliation. Revelation always has the effect of reconciliation. As we've just discussed, God's ministry is to bring life from death. Because God is the fullness of life, when God enters into the nothingness of death in God's revelation, death is overcome and life is brought forth from God's very person. Therefore, mission and gospel are linked further, for both are for the purpose of reconciliation. The good news of the gospel is that we have been reconciled to God (Romans 5:10),

---

19. Ray Anderson explains, "Why did the Lord wait until Moses was eighty years old, a failure and fugitive, with no possibilities? Because the element of human possibility must be removed. The people were powerless and helpless. They cried out to the Lord. Moses was chosen to be the redeemer because he was also without power on the human level. Moses understood that this 'powerlessness' is itself a necessary ingredient in the chemistry of divine grace." *The Soul of Ministry,* 45.

that we have been given new life by the God who has overcome death. Mission is witnessing in word and act to the fact that we have been reconciled—that God has revealed Godself and, in so doing, has taken death onto Godself, so what we might find life in God (John 3:14).[20]

Missional evangelism is not a chest-beating fight to prove who's right, an effort to convince people that they need to make a decision for Jesus. Rather, when evangelistic mission is seen in light of God's act of revelation and reconciliation, then conversion becomes the admitting of what is true. It becomes the acknowledgement of the gospel, the acknowledgement that you have surely been reconciled to God, that you have found new community with God. And this is possible because God (not you) has acted to reconcile you to Godself through your own and the world's *nothingness*, revealing Godself next to your yearning humanity, taking your death so you might live. Conversion is seeking to live into the new reality of God's act, opening one's eyes to see God revealed in the hidden and backward, and trusting the promise that God has reconciled you by overcoming death by making Godself known in death (John 5:24).

Youth ministry has tended to see evangelism through the lens of cognitive acceptance of the knowledge of the gospel; therefore, mission is the evangelistic impulse to get people to accept the gospel, both cognitively and emotionally. But evangelism and conversion are not primarily about our choices or decisions. They are about God's own action of claiming us, coming near to us, and making a way for us to be free from death (sin). We repent

---

20. Barth says it beautifully: "As creation is creation *ex nihilo*, so reconciliation is the raising of the dead. As we owe life to God the Creator, so we owe eternal life to God the Reconciler." *Church Dogmatics* I.1, 413.

for the ways we serve death, participating in sin as opposed to God's missional action. We'll pick up on repentance and sin more in book two. But for now, it is helpful to remember that it is the groaning of the Israelites, not their acceptance of any particular belief system, that moves God to act (Exodus 6:5). The Israelites, who are stubborn and would rather stay in slavery, at least cognitively and emotionally, are apprehended and converted not because a better and more convincing argument has been made but because God has acted next to and through their *ex nihilo*, through their deepest suffering.

Then, when someone encounters God's action of revelation, they are led through judgment by grace into reconciliation. Through our own *ex nihilo* (barren womb, stuttering wondering, impotence), God brings new life to us; God brings redemption and freedom. Evangelism in youth ministry is the proclamation that young people have been reconciled to God because God has acted for them. God has revealed Godself next to their deepest yearnings, questions, and brokenness. Because the gospel is revealed and proclaimed here, it is always humanizing and loving. Proclamation that is aggressive and forceful seeks reconciliation outside of how and where God reveals Godself.

Revelation is the revealing of the heart of God, while reconciliation is the invitation to live from this heart of love, to live in this new reality, where God makes Godself known in hidden and backward ways for the sake of new life in the love of God. We can see that the invitation that persuades the Israelites to follow God out of Egypt is not logical or cognitive. It is not the victor in a battle of ideas; it is not the promise of a more successful future. (This becomes especially clear after forty years of wandering.) Rather, the invitation is to admit and live as if you are reconciled, an invitation born in the very revelation of God, in God's coming near and seeking life within your brokenness.

PROCLAMATION

Proclamation and reconciliation then are linked; just as relational place-sharing is intertwined with revelation (as I said above).[21] God is revealed as the one who responds to suffering and groaning. God is with and for us. And God has reconciled us by taking our death, making it God's own, and overcoming it with life. Death (sin) is overcome, we are reconciled, and a new reality has been inaugurated (2 Corinthians 5:17). This reality must be proclaimed—and it must be proclaimed next to those raw places where God reveals Godself, next to our suffering and groaning, next to our experiences of death.

Gospel and mission both live from the act of proclamation. God proclaims, "I am the God of your fathers." Moses proclaims to the Pharaoh, "God says, 'Let my people go'" (Exodus 9:1). In so doing, Moses proclaims the good news of God's action.

If youth ministry is for participating in the act of God, then youth ministry will always be about proclamation. There will always be reason to proclaim the gospel to young people. It is theologically untenable for youth ministry to focus only on being with kids without also proclaiming in both word and act the new reality of God's reconciliation, of God's freeing us from

---

21. Place-sharing is the action of being with and for young people for the sole purpose of encountering their humanity, confessing that in so doing God is present, because God's action (in revelation and reconciliation) seeks to be with and for us. For more on place-sharing see my works *Revisiting Relational Youth Ministry* (Downers Grove, IL: Intervarsity, 2007) and *Relationships Unfiltered* (Grand Rapids, MI: Zondervan, 2009).

death. But this proclamation must take its lead from the very revelation of God; it must be the proclamation of the good news of God's mission to place us back in relationship with God not despite our yearnings, but through them. This essential proclamation in youth ministry demands the sensitivity of seeing the humanity of each young person, of respecting his or her deep yearnings and most profound sufferings—not because it's therapeutically appropriate, but because the God of the burning bush is a God revealed in the nothingness of our lives.

As Nadia pulled into a parking spot at church, all this was running through her mind. She felt like she'd come to a new understanding of her role. She couldn't really articulate exactly what had changed, but nevertheless she knew it. It wasn't like she'd mastered some new information; it was more that she felt she was being drawn into something. "I think I know what ministry is!" she said to herself as she slammed her door and walked toward her office. "It's all about proclaiming the altogether new reality of God's act of reconciliation. My job is to proclaim God's mission as the gospel. Youth ministry is not about getting kids to 'accept' the gospel," she thought. "It's about helping them see and participate in God's mission as the gospel. It is inviting them to see God revealed in their deepest yearnings and to participate with God as God brings life out of death in their lives, and in the whole of creation."

Nadia realized in that moment that she didn't need to choose Evan's emphasis on mission or Mrs. Davis's focus on church kids getting the gospel. Rather, ministry was about both gospel and mission, because ministry was bound within the act of God as revelation and reconciliation. Nadia would reach out to young people in the community not with a vision of converting them all, but with the desire to be near to them as God is near them. She would proclaim by her presence in their experiences of nothingness the profound truth of God's act of reconciliation.

As for Mrs. Davis's concerns that her daughter and the other church kids would see the wonder of the gospel, Nadia realized this could happen only if they saw the gospel through the very action of God's mission. The gospel would matter to them only if it were the articulation of a living God who was moving in the world next to their own and the world's nothingness. Only by participating in God's action of mission through revelation and reconciliation could they live into the truth of the gospel.

THE DRAMA CONTINUES . . .

By the time she reached her office, Nadia's time of deep reflection was over. Awaiting her were three sticky notes of bulleted to-do's. It was time to make retreat arrangements and return some parents' phone calls, among other things. She felt freedom, joy, and deep purpose in the knowledge that she was somehow in the mystery of God participating in the act of God. But now it was time to get some tasks finished and off her plate.

She was halfway through her list, when a great storm blew through her door—a great storm wearing a blue and purple Hawaiian shirt. It was Jerry, the energetic senior pastor. Jerry had a habit of barging into people's offices. It was nearly always done out of excitement (and never maliciously), but nevertheless, after a few dozen times, it did get old.

"Whatcha doing?" Jerry asked, patting her on the shoulder repeatedly. It was clear he had something on his mind.

"Do you want to talk, Jerry?" Nadia asked playfully, without taking her eyes off her computer screen.

"Oh, yeah," Jerry said, "I've got something to ask of ya." Jerry backed up and leaned against the wall.

Nadia turned from her desk to give Jerry her full attention, interested in what he needed. She could see immediately that Jerry was serious—something unusual for him. "Well, Nadia," Jerry said, his eyes turning from playful to stern, "you know we have a few budget shortfalls, and as you know I'm completely committed to not making *any* staff cuts, and I'm especially committed to youth ministry." Nadia's heart began pounding in her chest; she felt worried. As she listened to Jerry speak, she was surprised to find herself thinking, "My gosh, I love this job—I *really* love this job." Nadia was amazed by her own reaction.

Jerry continued, "The church council has asked the staff to do a few things to make sure we are using our resources wisely. They'd like every staff person to write up what they do and how it fits into the vision statement of the church. Can you do that?"

"Yes, sure," Nadia responded quietly.

"Of course, I did tell them a bit about what you do," Jerry said. "I told them you're really the pastor to the kids, and we need that. We need someone who has the know-how to pass on the faith to our kids. We definitely need that kind of expert!"

Nadia just stared back. Something wasn't sitting well with her.

chapter six

What Is a
Youth Minister?

As Jerry left Nadia thought to herself, "Is that what my job is all about? Am I pastor to the kids? And do parents think my job is to pass the faith on to *their* children, because I'm the 'expert'?"

As Nadia sat, feeling both anxiety about the potential financial problems and perplexed by Jerry's description of her job, the "ping" of her email went off, alerting her that a new email was in her inbox. It was Martha, Jerry's administrative assistant. The email read, "Nadia, we'll need that report in two days. Stay blessed, Martha."

Nadia had already done some deep thinking about what youth ministry was for and why theology mattered in youth ministry. She now felt pushed to think all these things through again, as she considered the question, "What is a youth minister?"

COMMON PERCEPTIONS OF THE MINISTER

Before talking more specifically about what it means to be a *youth* minister, it's worth considering in a more general way what it means to be a minister or pastor. Historically, there have been two common (mis)understandings of what a pastor is.

Distinct in Essence

One perspective thinks of pastors as somehow different in essence from others in the church. It's as if something is added by God when a person is ordained or called into a ministry position, something that sets the person apart, changing his or her whole person so the pastor can preach the word or administer the sacraments. It is like so many superhero stories when the gamma rays or the radioactive spider transforms a normal person from the inside out. It's often been assumed that the pastor or priest is different from the rest of the congregation in his or her (usually his) very essence. He may be human, but his humanity is somehow set apart and is therefore different (often assumed to be more holy) than the *common* congregation member.

The Protestant Reformation sought in many ways to end such a perspective. The Reformers recognized that this belief that only those with a distinct essence could forgive sins could easily be abused, such as when common folk were charged for absolution. They contended that there was very little biblical or theological grounding for this belief that a pastor or priest was different in his or her essence from other congregation members. But this thinking lives on. Some pastors still fear they might corrupt their holy essence by participating in questionable activities, or see their ordination certificates as giving them rights that are distinct from the rest of the church community. I once worked in a church where the ordained pastor had to drive three hours to administer communion to ninth graders on their retreat, even though a number of faithful believers and even a seminary-trained youth worker were already present. Neither the pastor nor the denomination that required this procedure would have said that the minister was distinct in his essence, but to all the young people and their leaders, it seemed clear.

Youth ministry has tended to avoid this danger. It is rare for the youth minister to assume he or she is distinct in essence from others—or for others to assume this to be true. (The very fact that most youth pastors tend to refer to themselves more often as "youth workers" is an indication of this.) Youth ministers (even when they are ordained) don't normally perceive themselves as clergy who are set apart from the rest of the congregation.

Now, that said, we youth workers have often had our own essence distinction. It has little to do with ordination and judicatory rites, but nevertheless has been a kind of distinction. Our essence distinction comes in the form of a perpetual playfulness, an extroverted personality, and a great deal of overall energy. We usually call these personality traits "loving kids." Those who possess these traits seem to gravitate toward youth ministry. We claim that a youth worker is just someone who "loves kids." Yet it's sometimes hard to distinguish between acting like a kid and loving kids. For many in youth ministry, our essential distinction is our kidlikeness. Of course, it's possible to lack these particular personality traits and still "love kids." But in youth ministry we haven't always seen it that way, and we've tended to think of our playful energy wrapped in youthful clothes as an essence distinction that's every bit as real as clerical collars and ordination certificates.

Nadia sensed that this was Jerry's perception every time she interacted with him. Jerry loved to remind people that he'd been a youth worker during seminary. Often, after doing something silly he would say, "See, my youth ministry days have never left me." Jerry wanted the youth ministry to have an electric energy about it, and often informally evaluated the ministry by whether he believed this energy was present. Yet the more Nadia thought about ministry as joining in God's action, the less satisfied she was with thinking that her role as a youth pastor was to be a playful, energetic person who connected with kids so she could connect them with Jesus. Even though this was what Jerry seemed to want, her theological turn would not allow her to go in this direction.

Hired Hand

The second way the pastor has been viewed historically is as someone with a function. After the Reformation, the pastor was less often perceived as being distinct from the congregation in essence and was more often seen as a servant of the congregation by virtue of his or her calling. The minister was a person employed by the church to perform the needed pastoral functions of the community. The control of the congregation had shifted from the distinct pastor or priest to the people. The people were the church, and they were the ones who called a pastor to serve them through particular pastoral functions (such as preaching, baptizing, communion, weddings, and funerals). Of course, the pastor still possessed some power as the leader of the congregation, but ultimately his or her perfomance was evaluated on the basis of how well he or she served the congregation by providing needed pastoral functions.

If there's a danger in this conception of the minister, it's that he or she is simply a hired hand, paid to provide a religious function. The pastor then is someone who meets the needs of the congregation members by doing pastoral things. Yet when the pastor is conceived in this way, his or her ministry can ossify around being a protector and propagator of religion, and his or her desire to continue functioning in the pastoral role can diminish attention on the action of God. The pastor can too easily become the upholder of a religious tradition, rather than the one leading the congregation into the action of a living God.

The hired-hand view is the much more common perception of youth workers. A congregation includes a number of young people to whom it wishes to minister, or sees young people in the community and wishes to reach out to them. When the church considers how they will do this, talk often slides into functions: "We need someone to lead a youth group," or "We need someone to start an after-school program." Having perceived this need, they look for someone to take on the function. Instead of the congregation ministering to its children and the children in its neighborhood, this becomes the function of the youth worker—it becomes his or her job. The church has hired someone to do its work, the work of passing on faith to the next generation. It becomes the hired hand's job to do the ministry while the rest of the congregation stands on the sidelines.

But this is where we have a big problem. We have argued throughout this book that ministry is determined by the very action of God. If the youth worker is the only one charged with ministry among youth, then not only does the congregation itself not participate in the action of God, but the hired-hand youth worker starts to perceive that her ministry isn't about participating with God in God's own act, but about being successful in the tasks of her job, building a big group with exciting events and great talks. And of course if these functions aren't present to the measure that the congregation desires then it can seek another, more skilled laborer to reach those goals. There then is very little about participation—either participation by the congregation in the ministry to and with young people or the church's shared participation in the action of God.

When she began her job at the church, Nadia thought of herself primarily as a hired hand. She saw her job through the lens of a trade, seeking to be a successful youth worker in the same way her cousin was a successful electrician. He got paid for doing the essential function of wiring houses and bringing them electricity. She figured she got paid for wiring the youth ministry with the electricity that could set young people's hearts aglow. She'd been questioning this self-understanding for months as she wrestled with the purpose of youth ministry. And after her conversation with Jerry, it was clear that this was his belief. That's why he thought it was essential that the church continue to have a youth worker: The church needed a youth expert on staff to do the work of wiring their children's hearts with faith. Jerry seemed to imagine that the church would not be functional without a hired expert to *do* youth ministry.

THE YOUTH WORKER AS PARTICIPANT IN GOD'S ACTION

But now that Nadia had begun the rich theological journey of exploring the purpose of youth ministry, she wasn't satisfied with the conceptions of the minister as either distinct in essence or as hired hand. It was clear that Jerry and others saw the youth worker from within these two perspectives. But both ideas had big problems next to Nadia's attention to the action of God.

Nadia did not find it helpful to think of youth workers as being "set apart" due to their playfulness and energy. It wasn't that she was against fun, craziness, and being playful, but these couldn't be the essence of a youth worker. If youth ministry is about participating in the action of a God who is revealed to us in the midst of our own and young people's nothingness, then youth ministry isn't primarily about energy and fun. It is about seeking God in the depth of the broken reality of our humanity, seeking the God who brings life out of death.

Similarly, neither could the "hired-hand" conception of the youth worker suffice. If youth ministry is about participation in the action of God, then it is not primarily functional but theological. Youth ministry isn't primarily about activities, but desiring to encounter the action of God in the lives of young people.

After his encounter with the burning bush, Moses saw himself as neither essentially distinct from others nor as a hired hand. When he returns to Egypt, Moses claims no distinction other than that in his broken humanity he has encountered the action of God. His only claim is that God had spoken at the location of his crushed humanity. He is not sent back to Egypt to free the people himself; it is *not* his job to do the functional ministry of liberation. Moses is called to proclaim that God is ready to move. The Pharaoh must let the people go, because God has heard their groaning, and from the groaning of death the God of life will move. Moses is no hired hand, but one who seeks to call the Israelites and Egyptians to prepare for God's mighty act.

Jerry's request had caused Nadia to realize that her job wasn't simply to do ministry among the youth, but to serve the congregation by assisting them in participating in ministry, providing opportunities for them to participate in the action of God by participating in the lives of young people. Nadia then, wasn't just a *youth* pastor, but a *pastor,* because her calling wasn't to do all the ministry herself, but to assist the people of God in doing the ministry. In the end, it wasn't her job to wire young people with faith. It wasn't even her job to pass on the faith to adolescents. This was the job of the whole congregation. Her job was to be one of the church's pastors by calling them to, and helping them with, the work of passing on the faith to their children and the children of their neighbors. Of course, her job will always focus on the youth, but her ministry was not to be isolated in concern for only the adolescents. She couldn't agree with Jerry's conception that she was the minister to the kids. Nadia believed she was called to minister to the whole congregation, advocating and assisting the congregation in participating in the action of God by seeing, hearing, and being with their own children, by passing on the faith to them.

But there was even more. Because Nadia saw ministry as participation in the action of God in young people's lives, she began to see herself as a local theologian. Her job as youth worker required that she be a theologian who sought for the action of God in the lives of young people, calling others to participate in God's action by being with and for adolescents. If through revelation and reconciliation God was found acting alongside the yearning and searching of young people, then part of Nadia's work was to see and articulate who this God is and where this God can be found next to the lives of young people and adults alike. To be a theologian is simply to reflect on the action of God, and to be a local theologian is to reflect on the action of God in the lives of specific people. To be a local theologian and pastor is to seek for God in the lives of these particular people while asking, What then shall we do? How then shall we go about acting?

THE CONCLUDING OF THE DRAMA (AT LEAST FOR NOW ...)

And so Nadia wrote her report. She boldly laid out how she saw herself as a local theologian, explaining how this perspective made a difference not only in her self-perception but also in her very action in ministry. She shared her view sensitively; she had no axe to grind. Nadia simply stated how her understanding of her own job as a youth worker was connected to her understanding of what youth ministry is. If youth ministry is for participation in God's action in the lives of young people, then being a youth worker is about reflecting deeply on God's action next to the lives of young people, while also calling adults to see and be with young people as participation in the action of God.

Nadia saw her job as participating in gospel as mission by assisting young and old to participate in God's action through their own and the world's brokenness. As she wrote, she realized how much time she'd spent struggling with the idea that her job was to build something—either to build a successful ministry or to build faith in the lives of young people. "No wonder I always felt frustrated and exhausted," Nadia thought to herself. But now, sitting in the middle of her theological breakthrough, understanding herself as participating in the backward and beautiful in-breaking of God, she felt only joy. She was thrilled to be in youth ministry because there is nothing more beautiful and wonderful, nothing more moving, than seeking for the God who speaks from the burning bush to use our impossibilities to send us into life in God's own action of love. Nadia was a minister of this gospel. Her job—her pleasure—was to dwell in this very reality with and for young people.

As she finished her report, Nadia shook her head, having no clue how it would be received. She felt a stab of hesitation and wondered briefly if she should just delete the whole thing. But it was too true, too close to her heart; this was what she really thought about who she was and what she did. As she told herself this, confidence swelled in her. It wasn't that she was sure her statement would be understood; in fact, she felt as tentative as ever about how it would be received. But she was filled with confidence and flooded with joy because she felt like she *knew*. She knew who she was and what she wanted for her ministry.

Nadia shook her head again, this time not in trepidation but in gratitude. She thought to herself, "What a gift, what a pleasure! I get to spend my life reflecting on and participating in the action of God. I get to be with a congregation and its young people, seeking along with them to live into this altogether new reality, seeking to bend our lives toward this new reality where God takes all that is dead and makes it alive."

"I'm free!" Nadia thought. "My job isn't helping kids be good, assimilate a tradition, or be servants. My job is to seek for the God who inaugurated an all-new reality in God's own action, bringing life out of all that is dead."

Her eyes filled with tears, and she said aloud into her empty office, "I can give my life to that!"

Questions for Reflection and Discussion

Chapter 1: The Chronicles of Nadia
- As you begin reading this book, how would you define the purpose of youth ministry?
- What expectations are there of youth ministry in your context? What expectations do you bring?
- How do you measure success in youth ministry? How do those around you mark success?
- What draws you to youth ministry? What do you love about it? What about it drains you?
- How has your own theological background, education, or preparation served you in ministry with young people so far?

Chapter 2: What's It All About?
- What would you identify as your intentions for youth ministry?

- How have you or others used theology to justify intentions?
- How do the three motives discussed (keeping kids good, involving kids in service, passing on the tradition) resonate with your ministry experience? What other motives might you add to the list?
- What are *your* motives for youth ministry? In other words—what is at your core that compels you into ministry?
- What prevents you from identifying or sharing your motives for youth ministry?
- How would you answer Mrs. Davis's question at this point? What is youth ministry for?

Chapter 3: Youth Ministry as Participation in God's Action

- If the core of youth ministry is participation in God's own action, what other motives for ministry need to be put to death?
- When have you found yourself in the position of Simon the Magician or Abraham and Sarah—attempting to call forth the Spirit or fulfill God's promises through your own efforts?
- How do you experience judgment as you explore the purpose of youth ministry and name your own motives? At the same time, how do you experience grace?
- What weaknesses can you identify and admit? How can you imagine that you might participate in God's action through these weaknesses?
- How would you define *theology*?

Chapter 4: How Youth Ministry Does Theology

- How do you understand the differences between theology and ministry? How are the two connected?
- Would you call yourself a minister, a theologian, both, or neither? What appeals to you about using each of these titles? What about them makes you feel uncomfortable?
- What has prevented youth ministry from reflecting deeply on God's own ministry? How can these obstacles be overcome?
- Reflect on the four priorities for doing theology as ministry (pages 60–71). Which resonates most with you? With which do you struggle most?
- How do you understand your own ministry among young people to be participation in God's action? As Evan put it: "So what do you think ministry is?"

Chapter 5: What is Ministry, Really?

- When have you felt, as Nadia did, "squeezed between gospel and mission?" What other terminology might you use to describe this tension?
- How would you explain the statement: "There is no gospel without mission, and there is no mission without gospel." to someone who understands gospel and mission as opposing and competing concepts?
- When have you seen or experienced God's action revealed in the profound, rather than the obvious, in your own life or the lives of others?
- If you were in Nadia's place, how would you respond, internally or externally, to Pastor Jerry's description of

you as an "expert" whose job is "to pass on the faith" to kids?

Chapter 6: What Is a Youth Minister?

- What is your definition of a youth pastor? How do you think others in your context might answer this question?
- Which (mis)understandings of a pastor's identity have you encountered or even ascribed to in the past? As a minister, when have been treated as if you were different in essence from others? When have you been treated as a hired hand?
- How do you think Nadia's new understanding of who she is and what she does would be received by those in ministry settings you've experienced?
- What new insights has this theological reflection on youth ministry brought for you so far? What questions have arisen or lingered?
- After reading and reflecting on this book, how would you describe the purpose of youth ministry?

A Theological Journey
Through Youth Ministry

Book 1: **Taking Theology to Youth Ministry**

Book 2: **Taking the Cross to Youth Ministry**

Book 3: **Unpacking Scripture in Youth Ministry**

Book 4: **Unlocking Mission and Eschatology in Youth Ministry**

Andrew Root

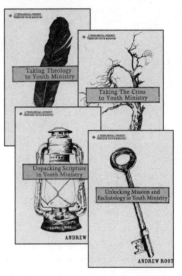

Even if you know you're called to youth ministry and are passionate about the students in your group, you've probably had a few of those moments when you've wondered why you're doing certain things in your ministry, or wondered why you're even doing youth ministry in the first place.

If you've ever stopped to ask, "What's the point of youth ministry?" ...

In this unprecedented series entitled, A Theological Journey Through Youth Ministry, Andrew Root invites you along on a journey with Nadia—a fictional youth worker who is trying to understand the "why" behind her ministry. Her narrative, along with Root's insights, help you uncover the action of God as it pertains to your own youth ministry, and encourage you to discover how you can participate in that action. As you join this theological journey, you'll find yourself exploring how theology, the cross, Scripture, mission, and eschatology can and should influence the way you do youth ministry.

Share Your Thoughts

With the Author: Your comments will be forwarded to the author when you send them to *zauthor@zondervan.com*.

With Zondervan: Submit your review of this book by writing to *zreview@zondervan.com*.

Free Online Resources at
www.zondervan.com

Zondervan AuthorTracker: Be notified whenever your favorite authors publish new books, go on tour, or post an update about what's happening in their lives at www.zondervan.com/authortracker.

Daily Bible Verses and Devotions: Enrich your life with daily Bible verses or devotions that help you start every morning focused on God. Visit www.zondervan.com/newsletters.

Free Email Publications: Sign up for newsletters on Christian living, academic resources, church ministry, fiction, children's resources, and more. Visit www.zondervan.com/newsletters.

Zondervan Bible Search: Find and compare Bible passages in a variety of translations at www.zondervanbiblesearch.com.

Other Benefits: Register to receive online benefits like coupons and special offers, or to participate in research.

ZONDERVAN.com/
AUTHORTRACKER
follow your favorite authors